Cooking to Beat the Clock

Cooking to Beat the Clock

delicious, inspired meals in 15 minutes

Sam Gugino

photographs by Dawn Smith

CHRONICLE BOOKS

SAN FRANCISCO

Library of Congress Cataloging-in-Publication Data:
Gugino, Sam.
    Cooking to beat the clock: delicious, inspired meals in fifteen minutes / by
Sam Gugino.
      p.   cm.
    Includes index.
    ISBN 0-8118-1860-8 (pb)
    1. Quick and easy cookery.   I. Title
TX853.5.G76 1998
641.5'55—dc21   98-4625
                                           CIP

Printed in Hong Kong.

Prop styling by Karen Quatsoe
Food styling by Marie Piraino
Designed by Helene Silverman

Distributed in Canada by Raincoast Books
8680 Cambie Street
Vancouver, British Columbia V6P 6M9

10 9 8 7 6 5 4 3 2 1

Chronicle Books
85 Second Street
San Francisco, California 94105

www.chroniclebooks.com

DEDICATION

to Mary

acknowledgments

I DEDICATED my second book to my wife, Mary Lee Keane, but I had to share my dedication with a co-author. So since this is my first solo effort, it seems fitting to acknowledge the most important person in my life.

Mary has stuck with me through thick and thin with support, inspiration, and sage advice for almost a quarter century. While my mother planted the seeds of my love of cooking and eating, it was Mary who nurtured the garden. Her first Christmas gift to me was my first formal cooking lesson. She encouraged me to take a comedy writing class at Temple University where I met my friend and mentor Art Milner. She's been a better editor than most professional editors with whom I've worked. And she has been a willing guinea pig for hundreds of recipes I've tested for my books and numerous magazine and newspaper articles. Mary deserves particular credit for the recipes that never made it into those books or articles. Those were the tough ones we tend to forget about.

I'd also like to thank the very professional people at Chronicle Books, especially Bill LeBlond and Sarah Putman, my editor Judith Dunham, my agent Jane Dystel, and the friends and family members who made up my team of volunteer recipe testers: Tina Phipps, Barbara Rice, Maryann Bolles, Stu Rubin, Maria and Skip Van Wie, Rosemary Ranck, David Traxel, Paul Laskow, Margaret Meigs, Ron Cole, Susan Dundon, Virginia Morris and John Morris, Faith Wheeler, Jeff Goldstein, Connie and Frank Oliva, Warren and Marie Potash, Traci Skene, Brian McKim, and Howard and Mary Hurtig.

CONTENTS

introduction

TODAY, the idea of Mom having all afternoon to prepare dinner for Dad's arrival at 5:30 P.M. is as dated as a Norman Rockwell painting. One wage earner has given way to two, and as often as not, both arrive home closer to 7 than 5:30 P.M. Even the kids have their own busy schedules. Time constraints are further compounded in one-parent families.

Everyone wants dinner ready in a hurry, yet one that is good tasting and reasonably healthful too. Take-out food has its limitations—how much pizza and kung pao chicken can you eat? And dining out can be expensive.

In a 1996 study commissioned by Land O' Lakes, fewer than 10 percent of those polled thought it was possible to make a successful meal in thirty minutes or less. Thirty minutes? That's a lifetime as far as I'm concerned. I know it's possible to beat the clock with a flavorful, nutritious dinner in fifteen minutes as long as you remember four concepts: Flavor, Organization, Focus, and Creativity.

These principles are the foundation of this book. They will enable you not just to pick out a recipe here and there, but to develop a lifelong strategy for meals that are fast, faster, the fastest you've ever made. Flavor means a pantry well stocked with ingredients that have great intensity of taste and texture. Organization means having the right equipment to simplify and speed up meal preparation. Focus means being single-minded about getting the meal out in a hurry and using laborsaving techniques to make it happen. Creativity involves strategies for preparing meals in minutes, thinking beyond recipes so you don't always have to follow a specific formula.

Of course, this book does have recipes, sixty very good ones. But you'll get even more out of this book if, in addition to using the recipes verbatim, you use them as a guide—the "teach a man to fish and he feeds himself for a lifetime" approach, if you will.

When I grew up in the 1950s and 1960s, a meal was a main course—roast chicken, pork chops, and the like—a vegetable, a starch, a salad, and often a dessert. Few of us eat that way these days, especially during the week. Most of the time we're satisfied with a one-pot meal or something similar, like pasta, risotto, or a main-course salad. If there is dessert, it's usually fresh fruit or store-bought ice cream.

Seafood Pilaf with Saffron and Peas, page 98

This book is geared toward the way we eat today. The dishes that follow are intended to be meals, not just quick recipes. So they are satisfying as well as varied and healthful. (Though this is not a health-food book, recipes generally use oil or butter in moderation and low-fat ingredients like turkey kielbasa. Recipes also contain a good deal of fiber from beans, vegetables, and grains.) Most of the time, the meal is served on one platter or out of one pot. With only a few exceptions, dishes serve four people.

You'll notice that the vast majority of the recipes are cooked on top of the stove. That's because the oven takes too long to heat up, though I do use the broiler on occasion. This strategy also keeps the house cool in summer. I use a microwave oven because it's a good time-saver for certain types of dishes, and because over 90 percent of American households now have them. But the microwave is not a primary cooking tool because I think flavors develop more in skillets and saucepans on top of the stove.

Another benefit of fifteen-minute meals is that cleanup is often easy because the number of ingredients and the equipment are kept to a minimum. Anything more elaborate would take too much time.

I don't use any special equipment except a food processor, which really isn't so special these days. And if you're wondering whether I have a fancy kitchen, guess again. Despite the fact that I've been a food professional for over twenty years, I've never had more than an average kitchen. No commercial stoves, no convection ovens. Rarely has my cupboard and counter space been more than barely adequate. Such is the case with my Manhattan apartment kitchen where the recipes in this book were cooked.

All the recipes have been tested to assure they can be completed in fifteen minutes. You may not be as experienced a cook as I am; I've been a restaurant chef as well as a cooking teacher. Certainly you're not as familiar with the recipes. So on your first try, a recipe may take fifteen to twenty minutes, maybe even a few minutes more. But once you get the hang of the concept, your speed will improve. (On the other hand, you may be perfectly happy with an eighteen-minute meal.)

That brings me to an important issue. You should never compromise safety at the expense of speed. Better to take an extra minute chopping that onion, than lose the tip of a finger.

Incidentally, the clock starts ticking on these meals after all the ingredients and equipment have been laid out on the counter or work surface, what cooking professionals call *mise en place*. The buzzer sounds when the meal is ready to be dished out. Since *mise en place* means equipment as well as food, it's important to read the *entire* recipe (not just the ingredient list) before beginning so you can see what equipment you'll need as well as familiarize yourself with the cooking methods. Even though you're under time constraints, the minute taken to read the recipe through will be well worth it.

This book is predicated on only one person cooking. But if a second person is available, terrific. He or she can set the table, open the wine, slice the bread, even make a salad if you want a more elaborate meal. These meals don't require any preparation ahead of time or any precooking whatsoever. (Though salad greens are washed within the fifteen minutes, it is assumed that other vegetables like celery or carrots have been washed ahead of time.) I do take some shortcuts, however. When using a dried pasta, I stick with capellini, the long and very thin pasta that cooks the fastest, and acini di pepe, the tiny pasta used in soups. I also use fresh pasta which, regardless of the type, cooks as quick or quicker. If you want to use a thicker dried pasta, like rigatoni, add five or more minutes to the cooking time.

With one exception, I use basmati rice exclusively because it cooks quicker than standard long-grain rice. If you prefer long-grain rice, add five or more minutes to the cooking time. Aside from one recipe that uses quick brown rice, I've stayed away from quick-cooking or precooked rice, but if that suits your taste, by all means use it. (Check the pantry section in the Flavor, Organization, Focus, and Creativity chapter for more detailed ingredient information.)

For the most part, this is cooking from scratch, using fresh ingredients as much as possible. I do use convenience items when the quality is good. For instance, canned beans are often very good, though the quality can vary from brand to brand. I also use roasted peppers in a jar and frozen peas for the same reason. Feel free to substitute fresh ingredients, especially in summer when produce is abundant. For example, when red bell peppers are cheap, you may want to roast a bunch in advance when you have some time.

However, this book is not dependent on cooking ahead. No huge pots of stew or gallons of pasta sauce made on Sunday are required to get a jump start on weekday meals. Every recipe is, as the French say, *à la minute*. Then on weekends and holidays you can cook at a more leisurely pace, say half an hour?

flavor, organization, focus & creativity

This book is based on four principles, which will enable you not just to pick out a recipe here and there, but to develop a lifelong strategy for fast meals, regardless of how long they take.

FLAVOR

Flavor means a pantry—which in this book also includes the refrigerator and freezer—well stocked with ingredients that, whenever possible, "do double duty in flavor and texture. That's what shrinks time," says Andrew Schloss, author of *Cooking with Three Ingredients* and an old classmate of mine at the Restaurant School in Philadelphia.

For example, with a richly flavored extra-virgin olive oil and an equally intense balsamic or red wine vinegar, you don't need much more than salt and pepper for a first-rate vinaigrette. Yes, you may have to pay more for these ingredients, but don't we always pay a little extra for quality and convenience? And isn't a superior-tasting final product worth it?

In addition to packing as much flavor and texture as possible, a well-stocked pantry means you're less likely to run out for last-minute ingredients, a double whammy if you're in a rush. Substitutions can also be made more easily with a full arsenal of foodstuff. Don't have pinto beans? Kidney beans will probably do. Chicken stock can sometimes be used in place of clam juice. Arrowroot for cornstarch.

The following pantry suggestions relate to the recipes in the book, though they have much broader uses.

Use them as a guide, adding or subtracting items to suit your own needs. For example, if you do a lot of Asian cooking, you may want to include ingredients such as hoisin or oyster sauce. Conversely, if you hate sardines, why keep them around?

ANCHOVIES: See Seafood, canned.

ARTICHOKE HEARTS: I prefer artichokes packed in water, which usually come in fifteen-ounce cans, to artichoke hearts packed in oil, so I can add the amount of oil and the type of seasonings I prefer.

BEANS, CANNED: An excellent source of fiber and nonmeat protein. Quality can vary among brands, especially for cannellini beans, which can be mushy. However, chickpeas are generally good. These two varieties and black beans make up the canned bean triumvirate in my pantry. I usually also stock red kidney, pink, or pinto beans and perhaps navy, Great Northern, or other white beans.

BREADS AND BREAD CRUMBS: Pita breads with a pocket, or the pocketless ones used in Middle Eastern Lamb with Cucumber Salad (page 40), keep quite well in the freezer. I don't like corn tortillas unless they're freshly made, so I use flour tortillas in San Diego Fish Tacos (page 77), Chicken Fajitas with Mango Salsa (page 54), and Huevos Rancheros with Spicy Black Beans (page 108). They will last a week or more in the refrigerator and can be frozen. (If you don't want them to stick together in one clump, separate the individual tortillas with wax paper before freezing.)

Fresh bread crumbs are always best but are not always possible to make. They also don't last as long as purchased plain and seasoned (often called Italian-style) bread crumbs, which keep in the pantry for at least six months.

BUTTER: I use unsalted butter because I think it tastes better than salted butter. Since it is more perishable, I keep one stick in the refrigerator and the rest in the freezer. Frozen butter defrosts quickly in a microwave oven.

CAPERS: The most commonly available capers are pickled in brine and come in two sizes. The smaller nonpareil capers from France are of better quality and are more convenient because they don't need to be chopped.

CHEESE:

Blue Cheese: Danish blue, Bleu d'Auvergne, or a good-quality domestic blue will work fine in recipes such as Pork Medallions with Cider and Mashed Sweet Potatoes (page 49) and Venetian Calf's Liver with Polenta (page 48).

Feta: There are several different styles of this crumbly sheep's milk cheese stored in brine, depending on where it is made. I prefer Bulgarian feta because it is creamier and less salty. American versions are usually made from cow's milk and are less flavorful. I store feta in a plastic container in the refrigerator where it will keep up to a week.

Goat Cheeses: There are a wide range of domestic and imported goat cheeses (*chèvres* in French) from which to choose, both fresh and aged. Fresh goat cheese as used in Shrimp and Goat Cheese Quesadilla with Avocado Salsa (page 80) often comes in logs. Coach Farms is one of my favorites. It even has a reduced-fat version. Fresh goat cheese will keep only a few days under refrigeration unless it is vacuum sealed.

Parmesan: The most versatile and important cheese in the world. Use the real thing, Parmigiano-Reggiano; it's worth the extra cost. Though freshly grated Parmesan is always best, for convenience buy it already grated (or grate a large amount yourself) and store it in the freezer, where it will keep for a few months.

Pecorino: A sheep's milk grating cheese with more bite than Parmesan. Locatelli is probably the best-known brand. Store it like Parmesan, already grated in the freezer, for convenience.

Others: For provolone, use the sharp, aged type, never the slicing kind. Aged Asiago and dry aged Jack cheese are alternatives to Parmesan. A sharp Cheddar or a type of Swiss is good to have for shredding or melting.

CURED MEATS AND SAUSAGES:

Bacon: Used in Spaghetti Carbonara (page 93) and Curly Endive with Pancetta and Blue Cheese (page 141), pancetta is Italian unsmoked bacon and thus has a more pure pork flavor than regular bacon. It comes rolled in pinwheel fashion and is available at butcher shops, Italian delis, and better markets. It will keep in the refrigerator for up to a week, but it can also be frozen. Slab bacon is a decent substitute for pancetta. Keep it in the refrigerator for a week (longer if unopened). Or better yet, freeze it, then slice off what you need for dishes like Clam Chowder with Potatoes and Bacon (page 115).

Canadian Bacon: Though it is often sold sliced, I like to buy this lean smoked pork loin in one piece so I can cut it the way I want, as in Quick Cassoulet (page 47). It will keep up to a week under refrigeration.

Prosciutto: Sometimes called raw Parma ham, though it is cured and ready to eat. Italian prosciutto from Parma or San Daniele (used in Pasta with Asparagus, Prosciutto, and Parmesan, page 91) has a richer flavor and is less salty than domestic versions. It will keep ten to twelve days under refrigeration.

Sausage: I keep at least one kind of cooked sausage in the refrigerator or in the freezer, usually Hillshire Farm's turkey kielbasa (used in several dishes, including Choucroute Garni, page 45), because it's low in fat. A number of companies like Aidells Sausage Company make a variety of flavorful cooked sausages with venison and duck as well as chicken and pork, all of which can be used by themselves or with pastas and other dishes. D'Artagnan sells several by mail (page 150). Cooked sausages will keep up to two weeks under refrigeration; fresh sausages, depending on the meat used (chicken is more fragile than pork), up to a week. Both can be frozen but the sausages should be individually wrapped so you can take what you need without mangling the entire package.

EGGS: Whenever eggs are called for in a recipe, use the large size. Always store them in their containers in the refrigerator, but not on the door, which is not cold enough. For people concerned about fat and cholesterol, egg substitutes work reasonably well in omelets or scrambled egg dishes such as Frittata with Artichokes, Roasted Peppers, and Pecorino (page 104); Joe's Special with Shiitake Mushrooms (page 107), and Spanish Tortilla with Baby Lima Beans and Potatoes (page 106). Those worried about salmonella in raw eggs can use egg substitutes for Main-Course Caesar Salad (page 139).

FRUITS, DRIED: Because much of their moisture has evaporated, dried fruits have concentrated flavor. Some, like Turkish figs and apricots, require soaking to soften up, so they aren't appropriate for quick cooking. For purely coincidental reasons, figs are the only dried fruit I use in this book, in Pork Tenderloin with Figs, Brandy, and Parsnips (page 50). I prefer the more intensely flavored California Calimyrna figs to black mission figs.

GRAINS:

Bulgur: Steamed, dried, and crushed wheat kernels now commonly available in cereal-size boxes in supermarkets. When sold in bulk, mostly in ethnic markets and health-food stores, bulgur often comes in two or three different grinds. I prefer the medium grind.

Couscous: Actually a kind of pasta, though used like a grain. It is almost always found in instant form but the quality is often good.

Polenta: Cornmeal mush that traditionally takes at least thirty minutes prepare on the stove with lots of stirring. Cooked in a microwave oven, however, polenta can be done in under fifteen minutes. Instant polenta takes only a few minutes on top of the stove.

Rice: With the exception of Lundberg Quick Brown Rice, which is used in Seafood Pilaf with Saffron and Peas (page 98), I use basmati rice exclusively in this book because this slender, long-grain, Indian rice cooks quicker than normal long-grain rice. It's also so fragrant and flavorful it doesn't need any embellishment. Indian basmati is available in many supermarkets as well as by mail order (page 150). Basmati is also produced in the United States as Texmati and in California by Lundberg. Long-grain rice can be substituted in many of the dishes, though it is not as fragrant or flavorful and takes longer to cook.

HERBS:

Fresh: Most major supermarkets carry at least several fresh herbs. I use mint, basil, thyme, chives, and cilantro most often. For parsley, I prefer the more flavorful flat-leaf, or Italian, parsley to the curly type. Fresh herbs will last up to one week, loosely stored in plastic bags in the crisper section of the refrigerator.

Dried: Though fresh herbs are invariably better than dried, they're not always convenient. Some herbs, particularly sage leaves (not ground), thyme, rosemary, mint, and marjoram, transfer their flavors relatively well from the fresh to the dried form. Oregano does too, but only Greek oregano, which can be purchased in bunches in Middle Eastern markets, or Sicilian oregano, which is similarly packaged and sold in better food stores. If you can't find either or can't get them by mail (see page 150), use dried mint or marjoram or fresh herbs. Stay away from what I call pizza oregano, that acrid stuff that comes in shakers in pizza parlors. Herbes de Provence, a dried blend that includes thyme and rosemary, is a terrific all-purpose seasoning. And bay leaves, an essential seasoning, are almost always purchased dried. When well sealed and stored away from the stove, dried herbs can keep from six months to one year, depending on their pungency. (Stronger rosemary, for example, lasts longer than thyme.)

LEMONS AND LIMES: Though technically perishable items, they're available year-round and keep well, so there's no excuse for buying the bottled stuff. Both will keep up to six weeks when well sealed in plastic bags and stored in the refrigerator.

MEAT AND POULTRY, FROZEN: Boneless steaks, whole pork tenderloins, veal cutlets, boneless chicken breasts, and turkey cutlets are good to have in the freezer. Wrap them in individual portions for easier defrosting.

MILK, CANNED: I keep a can of evaporated milk on hand in case I run out of milk or cream for cooking. Coconut milk, which is not a dairy product despite its name, is great for quick curry dishes like Chicken Curry with Tropical Fruit and Basmati Rice (page 58). There is also a reduced-fat version (coconut milk is high in fat), which I think works well.

MUSTARD: Find a Dijon style you like and stick with it. Depending on space considerations, you may also want to consider a coarse-grain mustard and flavored mustards, especially hot and sweet and green peppercorn.

NUTS AND SEEDS: While I often cook with nuts, I use them more sparingly for quick cooking because they are generally best when toasted, and that takes time! Some seeds, like sesame, can be toasted in a few minutes on top of the stove. Walnuts and pecans can be used without toasting. Buy pieces instead of halves;

they're cheaper and don't need much chopping. Tightly sealed at room temperature, nuts and seeds stay fresh for up to six weeks. They last longer when refrigerated (up to four months) or frozen (up to six months), both good ideas in summer.

OILS:

Nut and Seed Oils: Walnut oil is the most common, but almond and hazelnut oils are also great in cold preparations—especially when fruit is used. Only one of these is necessary to keep in your pantry. I especially like those from Loriva, which have a rich, toasted flavor (as does the company's peanut oil). Toasted sesame oil is a great flavor enhancer in Asian dishes; a little goes a long way.

Olive Oil: Use the more flavorful extra-virgin type in cold preparations like salads, or in cooked dishes where the oil is drizzled in at the very end to enhance the flavor. Find the specific oil you like, regardless of where it comes from, by experimenting, much like tasting wine. Always go for intense flavor. For sautéing or frying, pure olive oil or a lower grade of extra-virgin is fine.

Other Oils: When a neutral cooking oil is called for, I use canola oil for its heart-healthy qualities and relatively high smoke point. There are also many flavored oils on the market, such as those with basil, roasted garlic, and hot peppers. These are obvious time-savers because you eliminate at least one ingredient. I like the Consorzio line in particular. Well sealed in a cool, dry place, oils will last several months or more. I'm not in favor of refrigerating oils. Better to buy smaller amounts and turn them over.

OLIVES: I use mostly black olives and I like to have two kinds on hand, one oil cured—that is to say, not in brine—like those from Morocco or Sicily, and one packed in brine such as a meaty Greek kalamata or Italian gaeta. Pitted olives save time and kalamatas can be found this way. So can jumbo green Sicilian or Spanish olives. Jars of small green pitted cocktail olives—plain or pimiento stuffed—and a chopped version of pimiento olives called salad olives are convenient because they keep in the refrigerator for several weeks or more.

ONION FAMILY: Though perishable, onions, garlic, shallots, and scallions are pantry staples because I use them so regularly and they are available year-round.

Any white, Spanish, or yellow onion is fine in recipes that call for cooked onions. Buy different sizes so that you'll have what is called for in a recipe. In this book, a small onion is about four ounces, a medium about eight ounces, and a large about twelve ounces. When a raw onion is needed, use a sweet onion like Vidalia, Walla Walla, or Maui—all of which have less of a bite—or a red onion, which is usually between a Spanish onion and a sweet onion in intensity. I store white or Spanish onions in the refrigerator—where they'll last several weeks—because the cold helps to neutralize the compounds that cause tearing when onions are chopped. Sweet and red onions should be kept cool but not refrigerated and consumed within a few weeks.

Whole heads of garlic will last several weeks without refrigeration if kept cool. When a clove is called for in a recipe, it should be good size one. Like garlic, shallots will last several weeks without refrigeration if kept cool. Onions mixed with garlic are a decent substitute. Scallions, also known as green onions, are not because they are too mild. The green tops can be substituted for chives as a garnish. In the crisper section of the refrigerator, they'll last up to five days.

PASTA: I use dried pasta almost exclusively at home because, in addition to being incredibly convenient, it is consistently good. I prefer pasta imported from Italy and choose from among several brands. American pastas have improved in recent years, so try different brands until you find the one you like. I use dried capellini primarily in this book because it cooks the fastest among dried pastas. If you want to use dried pasta other than capellini, it will take longer to cook. Fresh pasta, regardless of the shape, cooks as fast as or faster than dried capellini. More and more supermarkets are carrying fresh pasta in a variety of shapes. While dried pasta, as the saying goes, lasts longer than most marriages, fresh pasta should be used within a few weeks if sealed and kept under refrigeration.

PASTES: Though they are not used in this book, prepared pesto, tapenade, and olive paste, to name a few, are handy for quick hors d'oeuvre spreads, pasta sauces, and toppings for grilled poultry or seafood.

RED BELL PEPPERS, ROASTED: Seeded and peeled and packed in jars, they are an essential pantry item because they can be used in pasta salads, sauces, and omelet fillings, and as part of an antipasto platter. Though expensive, the Spanish piquillo sweet red peppers, which are roasted over a wood fire, are sensational, velvety, and full of flavor. Available at specialty stores or by mail (page 150).

SALSAS AND CHUTNEYS: Both offer intense and multiple flavors that can enhance a sauce or dressing, or they can be served on their own to dress up a plain grilled piece of meat, chicken, or fish. There are a lot of mediocre salsas on the market, so be selective when choosing one for a recipe like San Diego Fish Tacos (page 77). For example, ingredients like tomatoes, onions, peppers, and cilantro should be high up on the list of ingredients. Indian and Asian markets offer a wider variety of chutneys than supermarkets.

SALT: I use kosher salt because it has a purer flavor than table salt and it doesn't clump. I keep it in a small sugar bowl for easy measuring, though more often I just grab some with my fingers.

SAUCES: If you use soy sauce frequently, consider having two kinds: dark soy for heartier dishes and a lighter soy sauce for light dishes and dressings. For those watching their salt, there are low-sodium versions.

Fish sauces from Vietnam (*nuoc mam*) or Thailand (*nam pla*) are great flavor enhancers—don't be put off by the smell—but they also have lots of sodium. Worcestershire sauce (made from anchovies and various other seasonings) is also worth having on hand. Sometimes all a dish needs is a splash or two of hot-pepper sauce. Tabasco is the most common, but I also like to keep a habanero sauce, which, despite its searing heat, has lots of flavor.

SEAFOOD, CANNED:
Anchovies: Most commonly available filleted and packed either flat in two-ounce cans or upright in jars. (Don't use fillets wrapped around capers.) I prefer the hand-filleted Ortiz Spanish anchovies, which are meaty and not very salty. They come in four-ounce tins and are available in specialty-food shops or by mail order (page 150). If you use only chopped anchovies, and not very often, anchovy paste in tubes may be more appropriate. It lasts several months in the refrigerator.

Clams: Minced or chopped (I prefer chopped) and packed in round cans, like tuna. After tuna, the most versatile canned seafood for chowders and pastas.

Tuna: In recent years I've switched from fancy albacore packed in water to light or albacore packed in olive oil because the latter has so much more flavor for everyday eating as well as specific dishes like Pantry Antipasto (page 136) or Salade Niçoise (page 142). Progresso is a widely available brand of very high-quality olive-oil packed tuna.

Others: Salmon, sardines, mussels, crab, and shrimp are not used in this book but are candidates for pantry stocking. For example, mussels could be used in quick pasta dishes (like canned clams) and sardines could be a part of an antipasto platter.

SEAFOOD, CURED: Smoked or cured seafood, particularly salmon, is a great choice for quick meals because it needs no cooking and a little goes a long way as in Capellini with Smoked Salmon and Scallion Cream Cheese (page 97). It will keep about a week under refrigeration and can be frozen.

SEAFOOD, FROZEN: I prefer frozen crab and shrimp to canned. The crab could be used in Corn Chowder with Crabmeat and Pimientos (page 113), the shrimp in Jambalaya (page 87).

SPICES: While ground seasonings are the most convenient, whole spices, like coffee in bean form, give more flavor and aroma when freshly ground in a spice mill, such as a coffee grinder used exclusively for spices. Specific whole spices I use are cumin, allspice, dried ginger root, black pepper (ground in a pepper mill), and nutmeg (grated with a nutmeg grater). I grind small batches of cumin, allspice, and ginger so I always have some that is as close to freshly ground as possible. Black pepper and nutmeg are ground as needed.

Other important spices in my kitchen include hot-pepper flakes, cayenne pepper, saffron (threads, not ground), curry powder, and paprika. I use less often Chinese five-spice powder, caraway seeds, chili powder, juniper berries, fennel seeds, and dried chilies (ancho, New Mexico, and reconstituted chipotle peppers in tomato sauce). See Mail Order Sources (page 150) if these less-used spices are not readily available to you. I keep a jar of pickled sliced jalapeño peppers in the refrigerator (where they last for months) as an alternative to fresh jalapeños. Though technically perishable, fresh ginger is always part of my spice pantry. To keep cut ginger from molding, wrap it in a paper towel and put it in a plastic bag in the refrigerator, where it will last a few weeks or more.

STOCK: A good homemade stock can add a rich flavor that canned stocks can't match. However, if you don't want to make an occasional pot of stock over the weekend, buy a good brand. Chicken stock is the most versatile. I like Health Valley fat-free chicken stock. There are also reduced-sodium stocks. Bottled clam juice is also very handy as a seafood or fish stock alternative in dishes like Fifteen-Minute Bouillabaisse (page 84) and Steamed Cod with Summer Vegetables (page 72). Just be mindful of its saltiness. Ditto for most canned beef stock. Canned vegetable stocks in various forms (such as low-sodium) are becoming increasingly available. Try natural-food stores and upscale markets if your supermarket doesn't have them. An alternative for canned or bottled stocks are "homemade" stocks in gourmet markets. These stocks must be refrigerated—usually for not much more than three or four days—but they can be frozen.

THICKENERS: I generally use cornstarch, but arrowroot is fine, though more expensive. Both work more efficiently than flour.

TOMATOES, CANNED: Canned tomatoes in juice are an excellent alternative to fresh for dishes like Fifteen-Minute Bouillabaisse (page 84). But don't always assume that Italian plum tomatoes are best. When I was food editor of the *San Jose Mercury News*, we did several taste tests of canned tomatoes, and supermarket brands did quite well. So shop around. Crushed tomatoes and chunkier diced tomatoes can save more time because no chopping is needed. Strained tomatoes are essentially a purée, and stewed tomatoes are diced tomatoes that are already seasoned. Stewed tomatoes can also have ethnic twists such as Mexican or Italian style. I find smooth and seasoned tomato sauce the most convenient, especially for dishes like Jambalaya (page 87) and Spaghetti Bolognese (page 94). Because you rarely need more than a tablespoon or two at a time, consider buying tomato paste in tubes, which can be refrigerated for several months.

VEGETABLES, FRESH: See Produce, page 29.

VEGETABLES, CANNED: In addition to those already mentioned, consider canned beets for the Pantry

Antipasto (page 136) or for a quick cold soup. Canned corn can be used in soups like Corn Chowder with Crabmeat and Pimientos (page 113). And sliced water chestnuts are good for stir-fries and salads like Asian Sesame Chicken Salad (page 145). For pickled jalapeños, see Spices, page 22.

VEGETABLES, FROZEN: Peas (especially the baby peas used in Scallops and Shiitake Mushrooms with Pea Purée, page 76), corn, broccoli florets, brussels sprouts, and lima beans (used in the Spanish Tortilla with Baby Lima Beans and Potatoes, page 106) are the frozen vegetables I use most often. Asparagus spears or cuts and frozen leaf or chopped spinach are also good to have around. Available in ten-ounce boxes or larger plastic bags.

VINEGAR: A great source of nonfat flavor in cold and hot dishes, and a good substitute for alcohol when deglazing skillets for a quick sauce in sautéed dishes. I use balsamic, sherry, and red wine vinegars most often. Balsamics come in many quality levels; the better ones are good enough to use as sauces or dressings by themselves. Raspberry is the most common of the many delicious fruit vinegars. Consorzio makes wonderful passion fruit and mango vinegars. Most fruit vinegars are less acidic than wine vinegars. If I want less acid but no fruit, I use cider vinegar or rice wine vinegar.

WINES, LIQUEURS, AND SPIRITS: Any alcoholic beverage you'd drink can be used in cooking, which leaves out those dreadful cooking wines sold in supermarkets. Rather than opening a bottle of white wine for just a half cup or so, I keep a bottle of dry vermouth in the refrigerator. Because it's fortified to a higher proof, vermouth lasts much longer, two months or more. Sherry has the same durability. You don't need a liquor cabinet of spirits, but a good brandy has many uses and can often be substituted for other spirits.

ORGANIZATION

Organization means a well-equipped *batterie de cuisine*, the right equipment to simplify and speed up meal preparation. You don't need anything fancy or expensive, but I recommend several items, some of which you may already have.

I can't imagine having tested the recipes for this book without my hefty twelve-inch nonstick skillet. A good twelve-inch skillet—or larger if you have the stovetop space—is the most important and versatile tool for fifteen-minute meals. It usually enables you to sauté enough meat for four people without crowding the pan. Crowding steams the meat instead of sautéing it. Large skillets also allow liquids to reduce faster for sauces because they have more surface area. More significant is the thickness of the metal. A heavier gauge metal (especially one with an aluminum core) conducts heat more evenly. This is important because you'll be cooking at high temperatures most of the time. A nonstick surface enables you to use less fat.

A wide surface area is also a good reason for getting a large, deep skillet (also known as sauté pan), one with a diameter of twelve inches and a capacity of four quarts or more. It should also have a cover and a short handle opposite the standard long handle for easy carrying to the table or counter. This larger capacity skillet will enable you to do braised dishes, stews, and soups in record time. Again, you'll want a heavy-gauge metal and preferably a nonstick surface.

I like to use nine- or ten-inch cast-iron skillets for frittatas and Spanish tortillas, the two omelets that go under the broiler. For breads like the pita breads in Middle Eastern Lamb with Cucumber Salad (page 40) and the baguette slices in Fifteen-Minute Bouillabaisse (page 84) that also go under the broiler, I use a shallow baking pan or baking sheet.

My wok has sat permanently on my stove for years, which should give you some indication of how often I use it. It is particularly good for fast meals because, in addition to being used for stir-frying, sautéing, braising, and steaming, it can be used as a mixing bowl. Invert the ring that comes with the wok so it sits closer to the flame, giving you greater heat intensity. I've found that electric stoves at full blast provide more heat than gas ranges.

I generally use only two saucepans, one with a two-quart capacity for rice and the like, and a larger heavy pan for polenta, risotto, and pilafs. For smaller jobs like warming the milk for Turkey Cutlets with Garlic Smashed Potatoes (page 66) or the liquor in Steak Diane with Parslied Potatoes (page 34), it's good to have a one-quart saucepan.

An eight-quart capacity pasta pot is essential, not just for pasta but for boiling, steaming, and poaching as well. Smaller pasta pots can boil over while you're performing another task. You might also consider a pasta pot with its own colander insert. That way you can easily dump the drained pasta next door into the wok and just as easily add some of the cooking water to the preparation, which several of the pasta recipes require. Failing that, a large, separate colander (about twelve inches in diameter) will work. When draining the pasta in the sink, I put a large stainless steel mixing bowl underneath to catch the cooking water if some is needed for the recipe. (Or you could quickly stick the pasta pot underneath.)

Though I advocate getting a butcher to pound meat like pork tenderloins or chicken breasts into medallions and cutlets for faster cooking, not all of us have that luxury. So you'll probably need a meat pounder.

This is a flat piece of heavy metal that may be round or rectangular and is attached to a handle (not to be confused with a toothy meat tenderizer). The side of a weighty cleaver will also do the job.

A salad spinner whips moisture from salad greens through the slats of an inner chamber into an outer chamber where it falls to the bottom. It works much faster than draining in a colander. For greens that are not particularly gritty, you can also soak them in the spinner, rather than using the sink. This also saves time.

A food processor is no longer a luxury. And for quick meals it's a necessity. For chopping and puréeing and for making no-cook sauces and dressings, a food processor can't be beat. I use the stainless steel blade 90 percent of the time but I also recommend using the shredding and slicing attachments. If you don't have a food processor, you'll need to add a few minutes to the preparation time for recipes that use it.

While the microwave oven is in over 90 percent of households, many people use this device only for defrosting or reheating. But the microwave does a good job cooking vegetables and it cooks rice, potatoes, and bulgur faster. (It also makes easy polenta, though not as fast as instant.) The microwave also frees up more room on the stove. Still, I don't use it extensively and I give conventional cooking methods as alternatives when I do. Most of my microwave cooking is done in a two-quart glass casserole with a cover that can be used on the stove.

You should have several mixing bowls, ideally a set of stainless steel mixing bowls with different capacities, including at least one that is quite large for fast mixing of main-course salads. In a pinch you can use a pasta pot or a wok.

The only knives you'll need are a sharp chef's knife about eight inches in length, a similarly well-honed paring knife, and perhaps a serrated knife for things like tomatoes and bread. It's important that knives always be sharp. Nothing slows cooking down more than dull knives. Most of us don't have the time to get our knives sharpened professionally, so I recommend a sharpening machine like Chef's Choice. Merely using a sharpening steel isn't enough.

Peeling, except for garlic and onions, goes a lot faster with a swivel-bladed vegetable peeler, especially one with a fat, easy-grip handle. For peeling garlic I use a garlic peeler, a rubber tube that removes the peel with a quick back-and-forth motion. (A rubber jar-cap opener can be substituted.)

Other utensils include a four-sided grater for cheeses and vegetables, a small colander or strainer for draining and rinsing canned beans, a heavy-duty can opener, tongs for turning meat, a wide metal spatula, a potato masher, a timer (preferably magnetized), a hand juicer, rubber spatulas, wooden spoons, wire whisks, a pasta fork, glass measuring cups for liquids, stainless steel measuring cups for dry ingredients, stainless steel measuring spoons, and a pepper mill. A few more things that are nice to have but are not essential: an egg cutter, which can be used to slice kiwifruit and mushrooms, a nutmeg grater, and a cocktail fork to extricate capers from a jar.

FOCUS

Focus means being single-minded about getting the meal out in a hurry. It begins soon as you walk in the door and put a pot of water on to boil and turn the oven to broil. Focus means the question, "How was your day, dear?" has to be asked and answered while *eating* dinner, not cooking it. No sipping of wine, listening to the news on the radio, or sifting through the mail. Get in there and get it done, then be as leisurely as you want afterward.

When I was ready to test each of the recipes for this book, my wife went into her office and closed the door. Then I set the timer and didn't look up until the meal was ready, fifteen minutes or less later. I prepared all of the meals myself, and having done so I honestly think it's easier for one person to handle the task, especially in a small kitchen. Two people can get in each other's way. Let the person who isn't cooking do everything else for the meal, from setting the table to opening the wine.

Though just about every cookbook tells readers to scan the entire recipe before cooking a dish, readers don't always do so. (I've been guilty myself more often than I care do admit.) Well, this time I *really* mean it. To make the recipes in this book work as quickly and efficiently as possible, you should read them through first. Most people know enough to get out the ingredients because they're listed, but they often fail to read the method for what equipment is needed. You don't want to be in the middle of a recipe and then go searching for a vegetable peeler or saucepan, only to find it is dirty in the dishwasher—or not find it at all. Remember that the timing of these recipes begins when all ingredients and equipment are laid out and ready to go.

Having equipment within easy reach is important. Because I often use the food processor, I keep it almost at arm's length. I suggest you do the same. That avoids rattling around in the cupboards. The same philosophy holds true for other equipment that you use often. Pots, pans, dishes, and utensils should be quickly available and not require a foot stool or deep knee bends to find. Put the dim sum molds, spaetzle mills, and other seldom-used items in the back of a drawer or in the far recesses of a cabinet.

Give yourself as much counter space as possible, even if it means putting a few things on the floor temporarily. My kitchen is so small that I routinely use the top of the refrigerator and the top of the microwave oven as holding areas.

Focus provides something even more important than speed—safety. Looking one way while performing a task in another direction is a recipe for injury. By being single-minded on the task at hand, you'll get it done quickly, enabling you to move on to the next one.

You'll notice that recipes will frequently say, "Meanwhile . . ." or "While the meat cooks . . ." This is simply a way of letting you know that at the same time you are actively performing a task, something else is taking care of itself. For example, in Panfried Snapper with Tomato Salsa and Basmati Rice (page 73), three things are going on at once. The salsa is being made while the rice cooks and the snapper sautés. You may be unaccustomed to managing such simultaneous tasks, but soon you'll feel comfortable with the rhythm. The Quick Meal Tips on page 29 will also help you to increase your speed.

CREATIVITY

Creativity involves strategies for preparing meals in minutes, thinking beyond recipes so you don't always have to follow a specific formula.

I realize that there is a certain comfort in following recipes. And I'm confident that the recipes in this book are good enough to be prepared again and again. Nevertheless, it's also my hope that you'll use the recipes as a springboard, a blueprint if you will, to create many more fifteen-minute meals on your own.

To do this you need to think about concepts, rather than specific formulas. For example, Beef and Asparagus Stir-Fry (page 38) is a meat and vegetable stir-fry when you break it down. If the meat isn't beef, it could be pork or lamb. Or it could be poultry, either turkey or chicken. Seafood might be shrimp, scallops, or cubes of tuna or swordfish. Vegetables might include string beans, broccoli, or several varieties of summer squash in lieu of asparagus. Obviously cooking times will vary, but you get the picture.

Chicken Fajitas with Mango Salsa (page 54) is a stir-fry wrap sandwich with a sauce or salsa. The filling could be beef, lamb, or pork accompanied by onions or bell peppers in colors other than the red ones called for in the original recipe. The salsa could be one made with tomatillos, jicama, or avocados, and the tortillas could be corn or whole wheat instead of white flour tortillas.

Add an ingredient here and there if it happens to be in the fridge or you just feel like putting okra in

Jambalaya (page 87). Maybe you want some red in Beef and Asparagus Stir-Fry. So you add some sliced red bell pepper. Of course, spices can be changed or varied in intensity to suit your particular taste.

Sometimes you might follow an ethnic bent. Say you're doing a pasta and you have fresh tomatoes around. Basil, garlic, olive oil, and Parmesan cheese are natural accompaniments. But you could just as easily go Greek with feta cheese, kalamata olives, and oregano. An Asian marinade for chicken breasts might be soy sauce, sesame oil, rice vinegar, and fresh ginger. A Middle Eastern twist could include cumin, garlic, coriander, lemon juice, and olive oil.

Once you feel confident, you might want to try some cross-cultural flavors, like Greek-style fajitas with the cucumber salad from Middle Eastern Lamb with Cucumber Salad (page 40). But go easy in the beginning. Don't just throw feta cheese and kalamata olives together with soy sauce and ginger. Even fifteen-minute meals have to have some logic and order.

quick meal tips

PRODUCE

Though I'm not a particular fan of baby vegetables, they do serve a purpose for fifteen-minute meals. Haricots verts are probably the best, for Salade Niçoise (page 142), Steamed Cod with Summer Vegetables (page 72), and Four-Bean Salad with Arugula and Red Onion (page 127). Also look for baby zucchini, pattypan squash, and eggplant. Small, new potatoes with paper-thin skins are not exactly baby vegetables, but they cook quickly and are delicious.

The supermarket salad bar may seem like an expensive way to buy fresh vegetables, but you're not going to use that much. Sometimes it makes sense to buy already-cut bell peppers, onions, celery, and carrots; cauliflower and broccoli broken into florets; and cleaned spinach.

Also convenient are the increasing numbers of packaged cut vegetables such as shredded cabbage for coleslaw and trimmed salad greens (usually called a gourmet or mesclun salad mix), just right for dishes like Duck Breast on Mixed Greens (page 69).

You can also buy cleaned spinach in bags in the produce section, though you'll still need to remove some stems and withered or slimy leaves. Still, you'll save time over whole bunches of spinach that need several washings to remove grit.

Better supermarkets and produce stores have already cut-up fruit such as melons, mango spears in jars, and cored pineapple. Use the mangoes in dishes like Chicken Fajitas with Mango Salsa (page 54) or Chicken Curry with Tropical Fruit and Basmati Rice (page 58). Pineapple can be substituted for one of the fruits in the curry.

MEAT, POULTRY, AND SEAFOOD

If you have a butcher, in a supermarket or in a real butcher shop, befriend him or her. Ask the butcher to pound pork tenderloins for Pork Medallions with Cider and Mashed Sweet Potatoes (page 49) or chicken breasts for Chicken Saltimbocca with Arugula and Tomato Salad (page 60), for example.

Though I don't use them in this book, some butcher shops and better markets have meat, poultry, and fish already marinated for cooking. My local butcher, for example, has pork tenderloins in two kinds of marinades.

Even without butchers, there are shortcut options in supermarket meat cases. More convenient than boneless and skinless chicken breasts are chicken tenders, strips of boneless and skinless chicken breast meat ready for cooking in Moroccan Chicken Soup (page 116) or easily cubed for Chicken Curry with Tropical Fruit and Basmati Rice (page 58). Larger turkey tenders can be used to make cutlets for Turkey Cutlets with Garlic Smashed Potatoes (page 66) or cut into cubes or strips as an alternative to chicken in stir-fries and other dishes.

Some supermarkets have bulk Italian sausage already out of their casings for dishes such as Spaghetti Bolognese (page 94).

Shelled shrimp saves a great deal of time but cooked shrimp not so much because shrimp cooks so fast.

Because thinly sliced prosciutto clumps together when you chop it, have the deli or market cut prosciutto a little thicker than normal. Then stack the slices to make it easier to cut them into strips for dishes like Pasta with Asparagus, Prosciutto, and Parmesan (page 91).

STORAGE

In summer, for cold soups like Endless Gazpacho (page 120), keep ingredients like tomato juice and chicken broth in the refrigerator so the soup can chill more quickly.

Conversely, room-temperature foods cook faster than those well chilled. Obviously, you can't leave a piece of meat out all day so it's nice and warm—and loaded with bacteria!—when you come home. But even taking foods out of the refrigerator as soon as you come home from work can help, especially if you're not going to cook dinner immediately.

PEELING AND CUTTING

When a recipe calls for a certain weight of potatoes, get the biggest potatoes you can find, unless the recipe specifies otherwise. Peeling and cutting one or two large potatoes takes less time than preparing three or four smaller ones. (The same holds true for onions and tomatoes.) To facilitate peeling potatoes, trim off both ends, then peel from the middle to each end all around.

The easiest way to peel, then chop or slice an onion is first to cut off a thin slice from the top and bottom. Then halve it lengthwise. The peel from each half comes off easily. With the flat side of the onion half on a cutting board, chop or slice as required.

When chopping or slicing by hand, always remember to turn the finger tips in. Use the large knuckles of your hand to guide the knife.

To chop a bell pepper quickly by hand, first slice off the top. Then stand the pepper upright and slice down inside the four walls of the pepper, separating them from the center core and seeds. Then you can cut the pepper into strips of any width and length.

For recipes in this book, salad greens are frequently cut with a knife. This will not cause rusting, as some believe, as long as you use a stainless steel blade.

Much of the chopping in my recipes is done in a food processor. If you haven't used this machine for chopping before, it will take a little getting used to but soon you'll be flying high. The principle technique is to put big chunks of (not whole) onion or cucumber in the bowl of the processor, then pulse, meaning to turn the machine on and off in quick bursts using the pulse bar. This prevents chopped onions from becoming onion slush. The second technique involves adding small ingredients through the chute (sometimes called the feed tube) while the motor is running. This enables garlic and chile peppers to be puréed more finely than if chopped from a dead start.

MIXING

Because they are more flexible than any spoon, your hands are the quickest, most thorough tools for mixing cold foods like salads. Just make sure you have clean hands.

Always use bigger mixing bowls than you think you need so you can mix quickly without the ingredients spilling over. Once combined, you can transfer the mixture to a smaller serving bowl.

COOKING

Recipes that use water to boil rice, potatoes, or pasta call for hot water from the tap. If you have a problem using hot tap water for cooking, use cold water, which will increase cooking time by a few minutes.

Most recipes call for cooking over high heat. This is how restaurant chefs can turn out meals in a hurry. In some cases I instruct the heat to be lowered to avoid burning. Since you can't do this easily on an electric stove, keep one burner on high and another on medium or medium-low (depending on what the recipe calls for). Then switch back and forth as needed.

Some seasonings may seem excessive, like four bay leaves in Clam Chowder with Potatoes and Bacon (page 115). That's because the bay leaves don't have as long to permeate the dish as they do in longer cooking. On the other hand, hot sauce will be full strength no matter how long it cooks.

SERVING

Don't be ashamed to serve food right from the pan. Hey, it's family.

MEAT

COOKING meat in fifteen minutes or less doesn't just mean running a steak under the broiler. Yes, steaks are good for time-saving meals, especially boneless cuts like the New York strip steak in Steak Diane with Parslied New Potatoes (page 34). (You could also use sirloin, tenderloin, or boneless rib-eye steak.) The Steak Diane demonstrates that you don't have to settle for a plain, broiled piece of beef. It is made faster by pounding the meat to about half its original thickness and cooking it in a hot skillet. Skillet steaks are usually done by the time most broilers heat up sufficiently.

I also like—in fact, I prefer—flank steak. This flavorful cut is the original cut used for London broil, which is essentially what Flank Steak Salad (page 36) is. (London broil is not a cut of meat but the name of a specific dish.) Flank steak is naturally thin, so it cooks quickly. In addition to London broil, it's great for stir-fries, like Beef and Asparagus Stir-Fry (page 38). Whether you slice the steak before or after cooking, it's important to cut the meat against the grain (on a diagonal) to break down the somewhat tough fibers.

Ground beef is good for quick dishes too, and it's used twice, in Chili with Beans in this chapter (page 39) and in Joe's Special with Shiitake Mushrooms in the Eggs chapter (page 107). I prefer ground chuck or round, but any ground meat cooks quickly, so consider ground lamb, veal, and pork as well. A combination of beef, veal, and pork might go nicely in the chili, for example.

In better butcher shops and by mail order (page 150), you can get game like venison and buffalo, both of which are extremely lean and should be done no more than medium rare—an obvious benefit for quick cooking—unless they are cooked with some kind of fat or liquid. You could try steaks of buffalo or venison in Flank Steak Salad or Steak Diane with Parslied New Potatoes, or ground versions of either in Chili with Beans.

Lamb has many of the characteristics of beef. For instance, you could broil rib or loin chops as you would a beef steak. I favor more interesting preparations. Middle Eastern Lamb with Cucumber Salad (page 40) uses a butterflied leg of lamb, which most supermarket meat cases have these days. It's essentially a large boneless steak. Pounding the meat will make the lamb cook more uniformly as well as more quickly. If your butcher can't do this, it is easily done at home.

Less expensive and somewhat chewier, though very flavorful, shoulder lamb chops are used in Smothered Lamb Chops with Orzo (page 41). This cut is more suited to the quick braising technique used in the recipe.

When I buy beef or lamb, I go for the best I can afford, usually prime, well-aged meat, which I purchase from a butcher because most supermarket beef and lamb is leaner, tougher, and less flavorful. My feeling is this: Eat red meat infrequently and eat smaller portions, but eat the good stuff. Don't be overly concerned about the fat unless it's fat outside the muscle that can be trimmed easily. My one exception is ground beef, where I usually go for leaner meat. Some cuts, like flank steak, are naturally lean.

I have reasons for using what may seem like a lot of pork in this chapter. First, pork is the meat that most often comes cured or smoked—meaning that it is already cooked—like the pork chops used in Choucroute Garni (page 45) or the Canadian bacon or kielbasa in Quick Cassoulet (page 47). Thus, it gives you a leg up on quick cooking. Even though ham steaks are not used in the book, they could easily be substituted for pork tenderloins in Pork Medallions with Cider and Mashed Sweet Potatoes (page 49).

Another reason for using pork is pork tenderloin, which is used in two recipes. This increasingly popular cut of meat averages about twelve ounces, just right for two people, and can easily be doubled to serve four. Pork tenderloin is also extremely lean, with half the fat of skinless dark meat chicken.

In Pork Medallions with Cider and Mashed Sweet Potatoes, I suggest you ask the butcher to pound the tenderloin into medallions. My recipe-testing volunteers have told me that a true butcher is more of a vanishing breed than I originally thought. When I retested the dish, I was able to pound the meat at home and still finish the dish in fifteen minutes.

There is only one organ meat recipe in this chapter, Venetian Calf's Liver with Polenta (page 48), because not everyone loves liver, especially kids. I've made the recipe for two, figuring Mom and Dad can eat it when Junior is at camp.

As I said in the Introduction, my hope is that this book can be used as a blueprint for many more recipes that you can create on your own. In this chapter many variations are possible. For example, lamb (perhaps cut from a boneless leg) or pork tenderloin could be used in place of beef in Beef and Asparagus Stir-Fry.

steak diane with parslied potatoes

One reason why this restaurant classic was cooked by waiters at tableside—other than to create a sense of theater—was it didn't take a lot of time. You can do the same at home, and you don't need to wear a tuxedo or diamond pinky ring. Just be careful when you flame the liquor.

Serves 4

16	**very small new potatoes, about 1¼ pounds**
1	**tablespoon vegetable oil**
4	**tablespoons unsalted butter**
2	**boneless sirloin steaks, 13 to 15 ounces each, pounded evenly to about half their original thickness (by the butcher if possible)**
	Salt and freshly ground black pepper
¼	**cup cognac or good brandy**
¼	**cup Madeira or sherry**
2	**shallots**
8	**chives**
8	**sprigs parsley, preferably flat–leaf**
½	**cup beef stock**

1 While the hot-water tap runs, halve the potatoes and put in a 2-quart saucepan. Barely cover them with hot tap water, cover the saucepan, and cook over high heat for 12 minutes, or until easily pierced with a knife. (Or put the potatoes and ¼ cup hot tap water in a microwave-safe container. Cover and cook in a microwave oven on high power for 10 minutes.)

2 Meanwhile, put the oil and 1 tablespoon of the butter in a large, heavy skillet over high heat. Season the steaks with salt and pepper. (If the butcher hasn't done so, pound the steaks between two sheets of aluminum foil or wax paper with the side of a cleaver or a meat pounder before seasoning.) Add the steaks to the skillet and cook for about 5 minutes (depending on thickness), turning once halfway through, for medium rare.

3 While the steaks cook, put the cognac and Madeira in a small saucepan over low heat. Peel and chop the shallots. Chop the chives and the leaves from the parsley sprigs.

4 When the steaks are cooked on both sides, remove the skillet from the heat and add the warm liquor. Making sure not to lean over the skillet, ignite the liquor with a match, preferably a long fireplace-type match. The flames will shoot up briefly and die down rather quickly. Have a skillet cover ready just in case.

5   When the flames subside, increase the heat to high, turn the steaks to coat both sides, then remove them to a cutting board. Add the stock and shallots to the skillet. Cook for 2 minutes, or until the sauce begins to reduce and lightly thicken. Reduce the heat and swirl in 1 tablespoon of the remaining butter.

6   While the sauce comes together, slice the steaks and arrange the slices on a platter. Spoon the sauce over them and sprinkle with the chives. Drain the cooked potatoes and toss with the remaining 2 tablespoons butter, the parsley, and salt and pepper to taste. Put the potatoes in a small serving bowl.

flank steak salad

The assertive greens and tangy dressing are a good foil for the beef in this hearty salad. Since flank steak is often twice the size called for in this recipe, cut it in half crosswise and make two meals out of it. The other could be Beef and Asparagus Stir-Fry (page 38). A cast-iron frying pan will give you the kind of heat you need for a nice crust. Serve this dish with a good country bread and a hoppy pale ale or peppery zinfandel.

Serves 4

2	**tablespoons vegetable oil**
1	**flank steak, about 20 ounces**
	Salt and freshly ground black pepper
1	**small bunch watercress**
1	**medium head radicchio, 6 to 8 ounces**
20	**cherry tomatoes**
1	**small sweet onion such as Vidalia or ½ small red onion**
2	**tablespoons prepared horseradish**
2	**tablespoons red wine vinegar**
6	**tablespoons extra-virgin olive oil**

1 Put the vegetable oil in a large, heavy skillet over high heat. Season the steak with salt and pepper. Add the steak to the skillet, cover, and cook for 5 minutes on each side for medium rare.

2 Meanwhile, cut off and discard the bottom 1 inch from the watercress stems and put the rest of the watercress in a salad spinner. Slice the bottom from the radicchio, removing the core. Halve lengthwise and, with the flat side down, shred each half lengthwise with a knife. Add to the salad spinner. Fill with water, drain, and spin the greens dry. Halve the tomatoes. Cut off a thin slice from the top and bottom of the onion, halve lengthwise, peel each half, and cut into thin half-moon slices.

3 Put the radicchio and watercress in a large shallow serving bowl or on a large platter. Add the tomatoes and onion. Put the horseradish, vinegar, olive oil, and salt and pepper to taste in a small bowl and mix well with a whisk. Add all but 1 ½ tablespoons of the dressing to the vegetables and toss well.

4 Cut the steak in half lengthwise (with the grain). Then cut each half on the diagonal (against the grain) into ¼-inch-thick slices about 2 inches long. Lay the meat on top of the vegetables and drizzle on the remaining dressing.

beef and asparagus stir-fry

Stir-fries offer endless possibilities for quick meals. Almost any kind of meat, fish, or poultry can go with a variety of vegetables. You can also add accents with canned vegetables like water chestnuts. This dish is a mainstay of the stir-fry repertoire. With the almost year-round availability of fresh asparagus, you can cook it whenever you like.

Serves 4

1	cup basmati rice
	Salt
1	flank steak, about 20 ounces
1	pound asparagus spears of medium thickness
2	tablespoons peanut oil
3	cloves garlic
1	1½-inch piece of fresh ginger
1	medium onion, about 8 ounces
2	tablespoons soy sauce
1	tablespoon dry sherry or rice wine
2	teaspoons toasted sesame oil
1	teaspoon cornstarch

1 While the hot-water tap runs, put the rice in a 2-quart saucepan. Add 2 cups hot tap water and 1 teaspoon salt. Bring to a boil over high heat, then reduce the heat to low, cover, and cook for 10 minutes. Turn off the heat and keep covered until ready to serve. (Or put the rice, 2 cups hot tap water, and 1 teaspoon salt in a 2-quart microwave-safe container. Cover and cook in a microwave oven on high power for 10 minutes. Keep covered until ready to serve.)

2 Meanwhile, cut the beef in half lengthwise (with the grain). Then cut each half on the diagonal (against the grain) into ¼-inch-thick slices about 2 inches long. Cut off and discard the bottom 1 inch from the asparagus spears. Cut spears into 1-inch pieces.

3 Put 1 tablespoon of the peanut oil in a wok or large skillet over high heat while you peel the garlic and ginger. Add the beef to the wok and stir-fry for 3 minutes. While the beef cooks, drop the garlic down the chute of a food processor with the motor running. Halve the ginger, drop it down the chute, and process until the ginger is completely chopped. Cut off a thin slice from the top and bottom of the onion, halve lengthwise, peel each half, and cut crosswise into ¼-inch-thick half-moon slices.

4 Remove the beef and season with salt to taste. Add the remaining 1 tablespoon peanut oil to the wok and add the asparagus and onion. Stir-fry for 2 minutes while you mix the soy sauce, sherry, sesame oil, cornstarch, and ¼ cup water in a cup. Add the garlic and ginger to the asparagus mixture and stir-fry for 1 minute. Return the beef to the wok and add the soy sauce mixture. Cook for 1 minute, or until the sauce is lightly thickened. Check for salt. Serve over the rice.

chili with beans

2	cloves garlic
1	tablespoon sliced pickled jalapeño peppers
1	pound lean ground beef
1	small onion, about 4 ounces
2	15–ounce cans red kidney beans
1	15–ounce can crushed tomatoes
1	cup beef stock
2	teaspoons ground cumin
2	teaspoons chili powder
	Salt and freshly ground black pepper
4	ounces sharp Cheddar cheese (optional)

1   Put a deep, heavy skillet over high heat. Peel the garlic. Drop the garlic and jalapeños down the chute of a food processor with the motor running. Add the beef to the skillet and briefly break up the clumps. Peel and quarter the onion. Add to the food processor and pulse until coarsely chopped.

2   Add the jalapeño, garlic, and onion to the beef. Cook for 2 minutes, stirring occasionally, while you open the cans of beans into a colander, rinse, and drain briefly. Open the can of tomatoes.

3   Add the tomatoes, beans, stock, cumin, chili powder, and salt and pepper to taste to the skillet and stir. Cover and bring to a boil. Uncover, stir, and cook for another 5 minutes. If using the cheese, grate while the chili cooks. Serve the chili in bowls topped with the grated cheese.

Most chili recipes stew for hours, but this one achieves a surprisingly rich flavor in a fraction of that time. Cornbread is a natural with this dish, but since it isn't normally found commercially, corn muffins or sourdough bread will do.

Serves 4

middle eastern lamb with cucumber salad

The cumin-seasoned lamb, cucumber salad, and grilled pita all combine to make this a midweek Middle Eastern feast. Try this with a syrah or other spicy red wine. If you can't get a boneless leg smaller than two pounds, cut off part and use it for shish kebab or cook the whole thing (which will take a bit longer) and use the leftovers for souvlaki sandwiches the next day.

Serves 4

3	**tablespoons olive oil**
1	**butterflied leg of lamb, 1³/₄ to 2 pounds, trimmed of excess fat and pounded evenly to about half its original thickness (by the butcher if possible)**
2	**tablespoons ground cumin**
	Salt and freshly ground black pepper
2	**cups plain low-fat yogurt**
2	**large English (seedless) cucumbers**
1	**clove garlic**
4	**large sprigs mint or 4 teaspoons dried mint**
1	**tablespoon red wine vinegar**
4	**pocketless pita breads, 7 to 8 inches in diameter**

1 Turn on the broiler and set the broiler pan so it is 6 inches from the heat source. Put 1½ tablespoons of the oil in a large, heavy skillet over medium-high heat. Meanwhile, rub the lamb with the cumin and salt and pepper. (If the butcher hasn't done so, pound the lamb between two sheets of aluminum foil or wax paper with the side of a cleaver or a meat pounder before seasoning.)

2 Put the lamb in the skillet, raise the heat to high, and cover. Cook for about 5 minutes (depending on thickness) on each side for medium rare in the middle.

3 While the lamb cooks, put the yogurt in a fine-mesh strainer over a bowl to drain the excess liquid. Peel and thinly slice the cucumbers. Put into a large mixing bowl. Peel and mince the garlic. Stack the fresh mint leaves, then roll and cut crosswise into ribbons. (If using dried mint, crush the leaves between your fingers.) Add the garlic, mint, vinegar, and salt and pepper to taste to the cucumbers. Mix well. Add the drained yogurt and mix again. Pour into a serving bowl.

4 Brush one side of each pita with the remaining 1½ tablespoons of the olive oil. Broil for 1 to 2 minutes, or until crisp and browned on one side. Meanwhile, thinly slice the lamb on the diagonal (against the grain). Serve the lamb on a platter. Put the crisp pita in a basket. Serve with the cucumber salad.

smothered lamb chops with orzo

1	**cup orzo or tiny pasta like acini di pepe**
2¾	**cups chicken stock**
2	**tablespoons olive oil**
4	**shoulder lamb chops, 8 to 9 ounces each**
	Salt and freshly ground black pepper
2	**cloves garlic**
1	**anchovy fillet**
1	**medium onion, about 8 ounces**
24	**small pimiento–stuffed olives**
2	**teaspoons fresh rosemary or 1 teaspoon dried rosemary**
1	**tablespoon drained small capers**

1   Put the orzo and 2 ¼ cups of the stock in a microwave-safe container. Cover and cook in a microwave oven on high power for 11 minutes. Keep covered until ready to serve. (Or bring 2 cups of the stock to a boil in a covered saucepan. Add the orzo, stir, cover, and return to a boil. Reduce the heat to low and simmer for 10 minutes, or until the stock has been completely absorbed.)

2   Meanwhile, put the oil in a large, heavy skillet over high heat. Season the chops with salt and pepper. Add the chops to the skillet and brown on one side for 2 minutes. While the lamb cooks, peel the garlic. Drop it and the anchovy fillet down the chute of a food processor with the motor running. While the anchovy and garlic purée, peel and quarter the onion. Stop the motor and scrape down the sides of the bowl with a rubber spatula. Add the onion and pulse just until coarsely chopped.

3   Turn the lamb and brown for 2 minutes on the other side while you coarsely chop the olives. Chop the fresh rosemary. (If using dried rosemary, crush the leaves between your fingers.) With a wide spatula, remove the chops to a large platter in one layer. Pour out half the fat from the skillet. Add the garlic, anchovy, and onion and sauté for 2 minutes. Add the olives, rosemary, capers, and salt and pepper to taste. Mix well.

CONTINUED

As a kid, Mom served us shoulder lamb chops simply broiled and served with a squeeze of lemon. These chops are just as quick to make because you don't have to wait for the broiler to heat up. They're also tastier. The lamb holds up well to the bold flavor combination of anchovies, olives, and capers.

Serves 4

smothered lamb chops with orzo

4   Spoon an equal amount of the vegetable mixture on top of each chop. With a wide spatula, slide the chops back into the skillet with the vegetable mixture on top. Add ½ cup of the remaining chicken stock (¼ cup will be left over if you're cooking the orzo on the stove). Cover and cook for 2 minutes over high heat. Reduce the heat to medium and cook for 2 more minutes. Serve the chops on individual plates with the cooked orzo on the side and the pan juices drizzled over both.

choucroute garni

2	**pounds sauerkraut**
2	**teaspoons caraway seeds**
3	**bay leaves**
½	**cup white wine, ideally Riesling**
½	**cup chicken stock**
2	**teaspoons juniper berries**
4	**smoked pork chops, about 4 ounces each**
1	**pound turkey kielbasa**

1 Put a deep, heavy skillet over high heat. Put the sauerkraut in a colander and squeeze out all moisture. Add the sauerkraut, caraway seeds, bay leaves, wine, and stock to the skillet and stir. Put the juniper berries in a tea ball or wrap in cheesecloth and put in the middle of the sauerkraut.

2 Lay the chops on the sauerkraut. Cut the kielbasa crosswise into 4 equal pieces and put them around the sauerkraut. Cover and cook for 5 minutes, shaking the pan a few times. Reduce the heat to medium, turn the kielbasa and chops, and cook 5 minutes, again shaking the pan a few times.

3 Serve the sauerkraut, chops, and kielbasa on a platter or right from the skillet.

This is a good meal to serve friends for an impromptu dinner on a chilly evening. What could be easier? Even the wine is a no-brainer, the same Riesling you used in the recipe. To reduce the fat somewhat, I use turkey kielbasa.

Serves 4

45

quick cassoulet

12-14	ounces turkey kielbasa
12-14	ounces smoked pork butt, skin casing removed, or Canadian bacon
1	small onion, about 4 ounces
3	cloves garlic
2	15-ounce cans navy, Great Northern, or other white beans
2	teaspoons fresh thyme leaves or 1 teaspoon dried thyme
1/2	cup tomato sauce
1	cup chicken stock
	Salt and freshly ground black pepper
	Hot-pepper sauce
1	loaf crusty country French bread

1   Put a large, deep, heavy skillet over high heat. Cut the kielbasa crosswise into 1/2 -inch-thick slices and cut the pork butt into chunks 1/2 to 3/4 inch. Add the meat to the skillet and cook, stirring once or twice, while you peel and quarter the onion and peel the garlic. Put both in a food processor. Pulse until the onion is coarsely chopped. Add to the skillet and cook for 2 minutes, stirring a few times.

2   Meanwhile, open the cans of beans into a colander, rinse, and drain briefly. Chop the fresh thyme leaves. (If using dried thyme, crush between your fingers.)

3   Add the beans, thyme, tomato sauce, stock, and salt, pepper, and hot-pepper sauce to taste to the skillet. (Go easy on the salt initially. The ham may be salty.) Cover and cook for 7 minutes, stirring a few times. Adjust the seasoning as desired. Serve in soup plates with the French bread.

I love cassoulet but it normally takes hours (sometimes days) to make. Not this one. Many substitutions are possible including making this an all-sausage cassoulet. It's also a good way to use leftover lamb, goose, duck, or roast pork from Sunday dinner, though neither the French nor I would ever use beef.

Serves 4

venetian calf's liver with polenta

Even if you hated liver as a kid, I urge you to try this dish, which is much less "livery" than you might imagine. But since some children would rather visit the dentist than eat liver, I've assumed this recipe will be made only for two adults.

Serves 2

1	**tablespoon olive oil**
1	**tablespoon unsalted butter**
1	**medium onion, about 8 ounces**
2	**pieces calf's liver, 5 to 6 ounces each**
1	**teaspoon salt, plus more to taste**
	Freshly ground black pepper
3	**sprigs parsley, preferably flat-leaf**
1	**ounce blue cheese, about 2 tablespoons**
¾	**cup instant polenta**
2	**tablespoons balsamic or sherry vinegar**

1 Put the oil and butter in a heavy skillet over high heat. Cut off a thin slice from the top and bottom of the onion, halve lengthwise, peel each half, and cut crosswise into thin half-moon slices. Add the onion to the skillet and reduce the heat to medium-high. Cook for 5 minutes, stirring periodically, until lightly browned.

2 Meanwhile, run the hot water tap and put 2 ¼ cups hot tap water and 1 teaspoon salt in a heavy saucepan. Cover and bring to a boil over high heat, 2 to 3 minutes. While the polenta water comes to a boil, cut the liver crosswise into strips about ½ inch wide and 3 inches long. Season with salt and pepper. Chop the leaves from the parsley sprigs. Crumble or chop the blue cheese.

3 Push the onions to the side of the skillet and raise the heat to high. Add the liver and cook for 2 minutes, turning once or twice to brown evenly. Add the vinegar and cook for 1 minute, shaking the pan to mix the onions and liver. The liver should be lightly charred on the outside but still pink inside. Turn off the heat under the skillet.

4 When the water in the saucepan comes to a boil, gradually pour in the polenta. Stir constantly for a minute or two with a firm whisk or wooden spoon until the polenta thickens. Reduce the heat to medium, add the blue cheese, and stir periodically for another minute or two until the polenta loses its grainy taste. Pour the polenta onto a serving platter or individual plates and spread the liver and onions evenly on top. Sprinkle with the chopped parsley.

pork medallions with cider and mashed sweet potatoes

2   **large sweet potatoes, about 2 pounds**
2   **tablespoons canola oil**
2   **pork tenderloins, about 12 ounces each, each cut crosswise into 4 pieces of equal weight and pounded evenly into medallions less than $1/2$ inch thick (by the butcher if possible)**
       Salt and freshly ground black pepper
$1/2$ **cup hard cider or nonalcoholic cider**
2   **tablespoons unsalted butter**
1   **teaspoon ground allspice**
2   **tablespoons brown sugar**
1   **ounce blue cheese, about 2 tablespoons**

1   While the hot-water tap runs, peel the sweet potatoes, halve them lengthwise, and thinly slice crosswise. Put the potato slices and $1/3$ cup hot tap water in a microwave-safe container. Cover and cook in a microwave oven on high power for 10 minutes, or until just tender. (Or put the potatoes and 2 cups hot tap water in a deep skillet or wide saucepan. Cover and cook over high heat for 10 minutes, or until just tender.)

2   Meanwhile, put the oil in a heavy skillet large enough to hold all the medallions in one layer without crowding. Put the skillet over high heat. Season the pork medallions with salt and pepper. (If the butcher hasn't done so, pound the medallions between two sheets of aluminum foil or wax paper with the side of a cleaver or a meat pounder before seasoning.) Add the pork to the skillet and cook for 7 minutes, turning once.

3   Remove the medallions to a platter. Add the cider to the skillet and stir with a wooden spoon, scraping the bottom of the pan. While cider reduces—about 1 $1/2$ minutes—drain the cooked sweet potatoes, retaining $1/4$ cup of the cooking water. Put the potatoes, cooking water, butter, allspice, brown sugar, blue cheese, and salt to taste in a food processor. Purée and put in a serving bowl. Pour the cider over the medallions and serve.

Cider and sweet potatoes signal fall for most people, and this great fall dish has both. Hard cider, an increasingly popular drink, has an alcoholic content similar to beer. But you could use a nonalcoholic still or sparkling cider. Drink what you don't use in the recipe with the meal.

Serves 4

pork tenderloin with figs, brandy, and parsnips

Figs or other dried fruit with pork make a great combination because the fruit marries nicely with the naturally sweet meat. I particularly like dried California Calimyrna figs but you could also use black mission figs. (Don't use the harder Turkish figs.) Prunes are a good substitute. Dried apricots are also delicious but they are chewier and need to be softened first by simmering in chicken stock or sitting in hot water while the pork cooks.

Serves 4

2	tablespoons canola oil
1	teaspoon salt, plus salt to taste
½	teaspoon freshly ground black pepper, plus pepper to taste
1	teaspoon ground allspice
2	pork tenderloins, about 12 ounces each
2	pounds large parsnips
8	chives
12	dried California Calimyrna figs or 16 black mission, 5 to 6 ounces
⅓	cup quality brandy or cognac
⅔	cup chicken stock
2	tablespoons unsalted butter
1	teaspoon ground nutmeg or mace

1   Put the oil in a large, heavy skillet over high heat. Combine the 1 teaspoon salt, ½ teaspoon pepper, and allspice and spread the mixture on a pie plate or wax paper. Cut each tenderloin in half lengthwise. Roll the 4 pieces of pork in the seasoning mixture. Put the pork in the skillet, cover, and cook for 10 minutes, turning once.

2   While the pork cooks, peel the parsnips. Thinly slice crosswise as uniformly as possible while the hot-water tap runs. Put the slices and ⅓ cup of hot tap water in a microwave-safe container. Cover and cook in a microwave oven on high power for 10 minutes, or until just tender, shaking the container once during cooking. (Or put the parsnips in a deep skillet or wide saucepan and barely cover with hot water. Cover and cook over high heat for 10 minutes, or until just tender.)

3   Meanwhile, chop the chives. Remove the stems from the figs and halve lengthwise (kitchen shears work best for both of these tasks). Combine the figs with the brandy and stock in a small bowl.

4   After the pork has cooked for 10 minutes, reduce the heat to medium-low and gently add the brandy, stock, and fig mixture. Cover, raise the heat to high, and cook for 2 minutes. Remove the pork to a cutting board. Let the sauce reduce and thicken slightly for about 2 minutes while you slice the pork.

5   Drain the parsnips and toss with the chives, butter, nutmeg, and salt and pepper to taste. Put the pork on a platter and pour the sauce and figs over the top.

POULTRY

BONELESS and skinless chicken breasts have been the biggest boon to kitchen convenience since ice cubes. Slap some prosciutto and sage on them, and you have chicken saltimbocca. Brush them with a mixture of soy sauce, ginger, and sesame oil, and they become chicken teriyaki. Slather them with yogurt and cumin, and you have chicken tandoori. Almost anything you have lying around the kitchen, from artichoke hearts to olives to roasted peppers, can dress up this otherwise prosaic but immensely versatile cut of poultry. This versatility, combined with their ability to cook so quickly, compensates for the fact that boneless and skinless chicken breasts aren't quite as flavorful as chicken legs and thighs, or even breasts on the bone.

To make quick cooking even easier, many supermarkets offer boneless chicken breasts cut into strips, often labeled chicken tenders. Tenders can be used for dishes like Chicken Fajitas with Mango Salsa (page 54). They also speed up cutting the chicken into cubes or chunks for stir-fries and for dishes such as Chicken Curry with Tropical Fruit and Basmati Rice (page 58).

Turkey cutlets are another convenience poultry cut, which most supermarkets carry. These slices of boneless turkey breast meat aren't as versatile as boneless chicken breasts because they are usually too thin to cut into cubes and are often not quite big enough for a single serving (at least for me). However, turkey tenders offer one more option. These boneless pieces of breast meat are larger than chicken tenders, about eight to ten ounces each. They can be sliced and pounded into cutlets for Fifteen-Minute Thanksgiving Dinner (page 64) and Turkey Cutlets with Garlic Smashed Potatoes (page 66). (One tender would make two servings.) They can also be cut into cubes as alternatives to chicken in stir-fries and dishes like Chicken Curry with Tropical Fruit and Basmati Rice.

Some markets also have chicken breasts marinated in different seasonings. I don't mind paying some-one to cut up and skin chicken for me, but I'd rather season it myself. You may feel differently, however.

As with ground meats, ground chicken and turkey—whether loose, in patty form, or in sausages—are options for fast cooking. Both can be used as substitutes for beef or pork to reduce the overall fat in the diet. But not all ground poultry is so lean. Some may include fatty parts of the bird unless the label says "ground breast meat."

I try to buy free-range poultry whenever possible, but that may not be an option for you. D'Artagnan and Polarica (page 150) sell free-range chicken and turkey as well as duck breasts by mail. Most good butcher shops have duck breasts. If you can't find them or don't have time to mail-order them, there are two alternatives. One is to bone out the breast from a whole duck (and use the rest for another purpose such as a traditionally made—not fifteen-minute—cassoulet). The other is to use an equivalent size of turkey cutlets. Since duck breasts are larger than chicken breasts, two duck halves will serve three people in the Duck Breast on Mixed Greens (page 69).

I stayed away from game birds for this book because I wanted to use mainstream ingredients as much as possible. If you have access to game birds, or want to order them by mail from D'Artagnan or Polarica, by all means do so. Squab or poussin could easily be used in place of Cornish hens in Chicks and Bricks (page 63), for example.

When whole breasts or, more accurately breast halves, are used, they are almost always pounded to at least half their original thickness to reduce cooking time. Ideally you should have your butcher do this. If that service is not available, pounding doesn't take very long. As with meats, boneless portions for poultry are generally five to six ounces. For meat on the bone such as the Chicks and Bricks, the amount is about double that.

Four years working in hospital food service taught me how important it is to avoid contamination from raw poultry. Rinsing the chicken quickly under cool running water and patting it dry before cooking helps to reduce some surface bacteria. In testing these recipes, I kept the chicken from my cutting board by working with it on the butcher paper in which it came wrapped. I like to have a small plastic bucket of hot soapy water close by to quickly scrub any contaminated surfaces, including hands. Every few weeks your cutting board should be sanitized with a solution of one-quarter cup chlorine bleach and two quarts of hot water. Taking a moment to be mindful of sanitation is just as important as being aware of safety when you're cutting and chopping.

chicken fajitas with mango salsa

This is an extremely versatile dish in which you can use turkey, lamb, pork, or beef instead of chicken. I like the hot-sweet nature of fruit salsas like the mango salsa. They pack lots of flavor with very little fat. If you want the salsa a little spicier, add more jalapeños. A great meal for kids.

Serves 4

1	tablespoon sliced pickled jalapeño peppers or 1 fresh jalapeño pepper
1	small sweet onion such as Vidalia or mild red onion, about 4 ounces
8	sprigs cilantro
2	ripe but firm mangoes
1	lime
2	tablespoons olive oil
4	boneless, skinless chicken breast halves, 5 to 6 ounces each, or 1 ¼ to 1 ½ pounds chicken tenders
	Salt and freshly ground black pepper
2	medium red bell peppers
8	fajita–size flour tortillas

1   Drop the jalapeño down the chute of a food processor with the motor running and purée. (If using a fresh jalapeño, stem and seed it first.) Stop the motor and scrape down sides of the bowl with a rubber spatula. Peel and quarter the onion. Add the onion and cilantro leaves to the processor and pulse a few times.

2   Place each mango, narrow side down, on a cutting surface. Slice through the mango as close to the pit as possible on one side, then repeat on the other side. With a teaspoon, scoop out the flesh from the two thick slices and cut each slice into 4 pieces. Juice the lime. Add the mango and lime juice to the processor and pulse just until the salsa is fully combined but still chunky.

3   Put the oil in a wok or large, heavy skillet over medium-high heat. Cut the chicken into strips about ½ inch wide and 2 to 3 inches long. Season the strips with salt and pepper. Raise the heat to high and add the chicken. Cut the top from the bell pepper. Stand it upright and cut down inside the four walls, separating them from the center core and seeds. Then cut the walls into thin strips. Add the strips to the chicken and cook, stirring periodically, for 5 minutes, or until the chicken is just done. The chicken should feel firm. (Cut through the center of one strip to check if you're not sure.)

4   While the chicken cooks, spread the tortillas on a microwave-safe plate and cover with a paper towel. Cook in a microwave oven on high power for 20 seconds. Put the chicken and peppers on a small serving platter. Put the salsa in a small bowl. Bring the food to the table for diners to make their own fajitas. To assemble, put ⅛ of the chicken mixture on each tortilla, top with a tablespoon or more of salsa, and fold the tortilla over. Allow 2 fajitas per person.

chicken puttanesca with polenta

Pasta with putta-
nesca sauce has
become a virtual
standard on restau-
rant menus, even in
restaurants that
aren't Italian. But
this spicy sauce
(puttanesca means
"harlot" in Italian)
can be used in other
ways—in a robust
seafood stew, as a
pizza topping, or to
jazz up otherwise
mundane chicken
breasts. Serve it with
an Italian barbera or
Chianti classico.

Serves 4

3	tablespoons olive oil
4	boneless, skinless chicken breast halves, 5 to 6 ounces each, pounded evenly to about half their original thickness (by the butcher if possible)
1	teaspoon salt, plus more to taste
	Freshly ground black pepper
3	cloves garlic
1	28-ounce can crushed tomatoes
20	pitted kalamata, gaeta, or other black olives (not ripe olives)
2	anchovy fillets
1	tablespoon drained small capers
1	teaspoon hot-pepper flakes, or to taste
1½	cups instant polenta
1	tablespoon unsalted butter
5	sprigs parsley, preferably flat-leaf

1   Put the oil in a heavy skillet large enough to hold all the breast halves in one layer without crowding. Put the skillet over medium heat. Season the chicken with salt and pepper. (If the butcher hasn't done so, pound the chicken between two sheets of aluminum
foil or wax paper with the side of a cleaver or a meat pounder before seasoning.) Raise
the heat under the skillet to medium-high and add the chicken. Cook for 4 minutes,
turning once halfway through, until both sides are lightly browned. Meanwhile, peel and
chop the garlic and open the can of tomatoes.

2   Remove the chicken to a platter, add the garlic to the skillet, and cook over high heat for
1 minute, stirring once or twice to prevent burning. Add the tomatoes, rinse the can
with ⅓ cup water, and add to the skillet. Cover and bring to a boil, while you coarsely
chop the olives and mince the anchovies. Add the olives, anchovies, capers, and
hot-pepper flakes to the skillet and stir well. Return the chicken to the skillet, reduce the
heat to medium-high, and simmer briskly, uncovered, for 5 minutes, coating the
chicken once or twice with the sauce.

3   Meanwhile, run the hot-water tap and put 3 ¾ cups hot tap water and 1 teaspoon salt in a large, heavy saucepan. Cover and bring to a boil over high heat, about 2 minutes. Then gradually pour in the polenta. Reduce the heat to medium and stir periodically with a firm whisk or wooden spoon for about 3 minutes, until the polenta thickens and loses its grainy taste. Stir in the butter.

4   While the polenta cooks, chop the leaves from the parsley sprigs. Spread the polenta evenly on a platter, in a shallow bowl, or on individual plates. Top with the chicken. Pour the sauce over and sprinkle with the parsley.

chicken curry with tropical fruit and basmati rice

The addition of fresh ginger gives commercial curry powder a marvelous flavor boost, and the briefly reduced coconut milk creates a luxurious sauce. You can substitute pork, lamb, or shrimp for the chicken and other tropical fruits such as pineapple for any of the fruits used here.

Serves 4

1	cup basmati rice
1	teaspoon salt, plus more to taste
2	tablespoons vegetable oil
4	boneless and skinless chicken breasts, 5 to 6 ounces each, or 1 1/4 to 1 1/2 pounds chicken tenders
1	2-inch piece fresh ginger
1	medium onion, about 8 ounces
2	tablespoons curry powder
	Cayenne pepper
1	14-ounce can coconut milk, preferably reduced fat
2	ripe but firm mangoes
1	ripe but firm large banana or 2 small bananas
2	ripe but firm kiwifruits

1   While the hot-water tap runs, put the rice in a 2-quart saucepan. Add 2 cups hot tap water and 1 teaspoon salt. Bring to a boil over high heat, then reduce the heat to low, cover, and cook for 10 minutes. Turn off the heat and keep covered until ready to serve. (Or put the rice, 2 cups hot tap water, and 1 teaspoon salt in a 2-quart microwave-safe container. Cover and cook in a microwave oven on high power for 10 minutes. Keep covered until ready to serve.)

2   Put the oil in a large, heavy skillet over medium-high heat. Cut the chicken into 1-inch pieces. Raise the heat to high and add the chicken. Peel and halve the ginger. Drop the ginger down the chute of a food processor with the motor running. While it purées, peel and quarter the onion. Add it to the processor and pulse just until chopped. Add the ginger and onion to the skillet and stir. Add the curry, cayenne, and salt to taste. Cook for 2 minutes, stirring occasionally. Add the coconut milk, stir, and bring to a boil. Continue cooking, uncovered, for about 5 minutes, or until slightly thickened.

3   Meanwhile, place each mango, narrow side down, on a cutting surface. Slice through the mango as close to the pit as possible on one side, then repeat on the other side. With a teaspoon, scoop out the flesh from the two thick slices and cut into bite-size pieces. Peel the banana and cut crosswise into 1/4-inch-thick slices. Peel the kiwis and halve lengthwise, then cut each half crosswise into 4 half-moon slices. Add the fruit to the chicken and stir gently. Cook for 1 to 2 minutes, only until the fruit is heated through but still maintains its shape. Serve over the rice.

chicken saltimbocca with arugula and tomato salad

Saltimbocca means "jump into the mouth" and is classically made with veal cutlets, though turkey is often substituted. Here I use chicken with equally good results. Make sure the prosciutto is not cut too thin or it will be hard to handle. Arugula is now available year-round, but it's usually too pungent in warmer weather. So this dish is best made in September or early October when things start to cool down, but local tomatoes and basil are still available.

Serves 4

4	tablespoons extra-virgin olive oil
4	boneless, skinless chicken breast halves, 5 to 6 ounces each, pounded evenly to half their original thickness (by the butcher if possible)
	Salt and freshly ground black pepper
1/3	cup all-purpose flour
4	slices prosciutto, about 2 ounces
2	small bunches arugula
1	medium to large tomato, about 12 ounces
8	fresh basil leaves
1	tablespoon balsamic vinegar or high-quality red wine vinegar
4	fresh sage leaves or 1/2 teaspoon dried sage leaves
1/2	cup dry white wine

I   Fill the sink with cold water while you put 2 tablespoons of the oil in a heavy skillet large enough to hold all the chicken in one layer without crowding. Put the skillet over medium heat. (If the butcher hasn't done so, pound the chicken between two sheets of aluminum foil or wax paper with the side of a cleaver or a meat pounder.) Season the chicken with salt and pepper. Put the flour on a pie plate or wax paper. Press a slice of prosciutto onto each of the breast halves, then dredge the breast halves in the flour, shaking off any excess. Raise the heat under the skillet to medium-high and add the chicken, prosciutto side down. Cook for 5 minutes on one side.

2   While the chicken cooks, cut the arugula crosswise into 1/2-inch-wide strips, discarding the stems. Wash the arugula briefly but vigorously in the sink to remove grit, then spin dry in a salad spinner. Remove any excess moisture with paper towels. Cut the tomato in half lengthwise, gently squeeze out some of the juice and seeds, and cut each half into thin wedges, removing the core as you do.

3   Turn the chicken over and cook for 3 minutes. Meanwhile, chop the basil. Put the remaining 2 tablespoons of oil, the vinegar, and salt and pepper to taste in a small bowl and mix well with a whisk. Chop the sage. (If using dried sage, crush with fingers.)

CONTINUED

chicken saltimbocca with arugula and tomato salad

4 Sprinkle the sage on top of the chicken, add the wine, and cook for 1 to 2 minutes, just until the chicken is cooked through and opaque. (Cut into one piece to check if you're not sure.) Remove the chicken to a serving platter. Raise the heat to high under the skillet and stir the wine often with a wooden spoon, scraping the bits from the bottom of the pan. Cook for 1 to 2 minutes, or until the liquid is reduced and lightly thickened to create a sauce.

5 While the sauce finishes cooking, put the arugula and tomato in a large mixing bowl, sprinkle with the basil and toss with the dressing. Pour the sauce over the chicken and serve with the salad.

chicks and bricks

¼ **cup canola or vegetable oil**
2 **Cornish hens, about 1½ pounds each, butterflied, breast bone removed, and pounded flat (by the butcher if possible)**
Salt and freshly ground black pepper
1 **small head radicchio, 4 to 5 ounces**
1 **head frisée or 1 small head curly endive or escarole, 8 to 9 ounces**
3 **scallions**
⅓ **cup walnut, peanut, or extra–virgin olive oil**
1 **teaspoon Dijon mustard**
2 **tablespoons balsamic or red wine vinegar**

1 Divide the canola oil between two heavy 9-inch skillets (cast-iron frying pans are ideal for this dish) over medium heat. Season the hens with salt and pepper. (If the butcher hasn't done so, butterfly the Cornish hens first by cutting through the backbone with a knife or kitchen shears. Then flatten the hens between two sheets of aluminum foil or wax paper with the side of a cleaver or a meat pounder before seasoning.) Raise the heat under the skillets to high and put one hen in each skillet, skin side down. Put a plate on top of each hen, then set weights on each plate, at least 5 pounds per plate. Reduce the heat to medium-high and cook for 14 minutes, turning once halfway through. When the hens are done, the juices from the thigh will run clear when pierced.

2 Meanwhile, slice the bottom from the radicchio, removing the core. Halve lengthwise and, with the flat side down, shred each half lengthwise with a knife. Put in a salad spinner. Slice the bottom from the frisée, removing the core. Cut crosswise into ½-inch-wide strips. Add to the salad spinner. Fill the salad spinner with water, drain, and spin the greens dry. Remove any excess moisture with paper towels.

3 Trim the scallions and mince the white parts and about 2 inches of the green. Put them in a small bowl. Add the oil, mustard, vinegar, and salt and pepper to taste. Mix well with a small whisk. Thinly slice the rest of the scallion greens, crosswise.

4 In a large bowl, toss the greens with all but ¼ cup of the dressing. Divide the greens among four plates. When the hens are cooked, separate each into two halves. Put a half on each plate, either on the greens or off to the side, skin side up. Spoon 1 tablespoon of the remaining dressing on each of the halves and sprinkle the scallion greens on top.

This rustic Tuscan dish, called pollo al mattone, *is traditionally made by weighting down chicken in a frying pan with a heavy weight, usually bricks—which is what* mattone *means. But anything weighty will do, like a mortar from a mortar and pestle, some large cans, or a couple of bowling trophies. The result is not only a dish that cooks quickly (something the Italians didn't necessarily have in mind) but chicken with a delicious crispness on the outside and a moist succulence inside.*

Serves 4

fifteen-minute thanksgiving dinner

This meal is for people who have to work on Thanksgiving and don't feel like cooking a traditional turkey dinner, or perhaps for people who don't want to cook a whole bird. Or maybe it's just for people who like Thanksgiving all year long. All you need is pumpkin pie.

Serves 4

4	**tablespoons unsalted butter**
2	**tablespoons canola or vegetable oil**
4	**turkey cutlets, 5 to 6 ounces each, pounded ¼ to ⅜ inches thick (by the butcher if possible)**
	Salt and freshly ground black pepper
⅓	**cup all-purpose flour**
1	**small to medium onion, 4 to 8 ounces**
1	**rib celery**
12	**ounces sliced white bread**
2	**cups warm water in a small bowl**
5	**fresh sage leaves or ½ tablespoon dried sage leaves (not ground)**
¾	**cup chicken stock**
1	**16-ounce can whole-berry cranberry sauce**
2	**tablespoons pecan pieces**
2	**tablespoons candied ginger**
¼	**cup dry sherry or brandy**
2	**ounces fresh white mushrooms**

1   Put 2 tablespoons of butter and 1 tablespoon of oil in a heavy skillet large enough to hold all the cutlets in one layer without crowding. Put the skillet over medium heat. Season the cutlets with salt and pepper. Put the flour on a pie plate or wax paper. Dredge the cutlets in the flour, shaking off any excess, and add to the skillet. Raise the heat to medium-high and cook the cutlets for 4 minutes on one side. Turn the cutlets over and cook for 4 more minutes or until the meat is firm and no pink shows in the middle.

2   Meanwhile, put 2 tablespoons of the remaining butter and 1 tablespoon of the remaining oil in another large heavy skillet (preferably nonstick) over medium-high heat. Peel and quarter the onion. Trim and cut the celery into 4 pieces. Put the onion and celery in a food processor and pulse until just chopped. (Or coarsely chop by hand.) Add the celery and onion to the skillet, stir, and cook for 3 minutes. Reduce the heat to medium.

3   Lightly dip 2 or 3 slices of bread at a time in the warm water. Squeeze out most of the moisture and coarsely crumble the bread into a large mixing bowl. Finely chop the fresh sage leaves. (If using dried sage leaves, crush them with your fingers.) Add the sage and

salt and pepper to taste to the bread. Mix well and add to the skillet. Cook for 5 minutes, until nicely browned and lightly crisp. Turn the stuffing over periodically to brown evenly. Reduce the heat if needed to prevent burning. Moisten with ¼ cup of the chicken stock and cook another 2 minutes.

4   While cutlets and stuffing cook, open the can of cranberry sauce and pour it into a small bowl. Coarsely chop the pecans. Chop the candied ginger. Add both to the cranberry sauce and mix well.

5   Slice the mushrooms. When the turkey is done, remove to a large platter and keep warm. Add the mushrooms to the skillet, raise the heat to high and stir. Add the sherry and the remaining ½ cup of chicken stock. Cook for 2 minutes, stirring with a wooden spoon to scrape any bits from the bottom, until the sauce is lightly thickened. Taste for salt and pepper. Put the stuffing in the center of the platter with the turkey cutlets around it. Pour the sauce over both. Serve the cranberry sauce on the side.

turkey cutlets with garlic smashed potatoes

"A real stick-to-the-ribs meal," said one of my volunteer recipe testers about this one. The cutlets remind me of the veal cutlets I used to love as a kid because they taste so similar. Both of them are great in sandwiches the next day. I call the potatoes smashed potatoes because they remain somewhat lumpy. Normally I don't use a food processor for mashed potatoes, but by pulsing the processor instead of letting it run wild, you can avoid the gluey texture that processors can give mashed potatoes.

Serves 4

1	pound large red-skinned potatoes
3	cloves garlic
1	teaspoon salt, plus more to taste
8	tablespoons olive oil
1	cup Italian-style seasoned bread crumbs
¼	cup Dijon mustard
4	turkey cutlets, 5 to 6 ounces each, pounded evenly to ¼ to ⅜ inch thick (by the butcher if possible)
1	cup milk
8	chives
1	tablespoon unsalted butter
	Freshly ground black pepper

1 While the hot-water tap runs, quarter the potatoes lengthwise. (No need to peel.) Cut the pieces crosswise into thin slices and put in a large saucepan or deep skillet. Barely cover with hot tap water and put over high heat. Peel the garlic and add to the saucepan with 1 teaspoon salt. Cover and cook for 12 minutes, or until the potatoes are just tender. (Or put the potatoes, ¼ cup hot water, garlic, and 1 teaspoon salt in a 2-quart microwave-safe container. Cover and put in a microwave oven on high power for 10 minutes.)

2 Meanwhile, put 7 tablespoons of the oil in a heavy (preferably nonstick) skillet large enough to hold all the cutlets in one layer without crowding. Put the skillet over medium heat. Put the bread crumbs on a pie plate or wax paper. Mix the remaining 1 tablespoon oil with the mustard in a cup. Using a pastry brush or spoon, spread each side of the turkey cutlets with the mustard mixture and press the cutlets into the breadcrumbs, turning to coat evenly.

3 Raise the heat under the skillet to medium-high, add the cutlets, and cook for 4 minutes on one side. Reduce the heat to medium and cook the cutlets for 4 minutes on the other side, or until the meat is firm and no pink shows in the middle. (Cut into one to check if you're not sure.) Reduce the heat further if necessary to prevent burning and turn the cutlets gently to avoid damaging the bread crumb coating. (A wide spatula is best for

this.) While the cutlets cook, warm the milk in a small saucepan over medium heat. (Or put the milk in a microwave-safe container, cover, and heat in a microwave oven on high power for 1 ½ minutes.) Chop the chives.

4   Drain the cooked potatoes and put them and the garlic in a food processor. Pulse a few times. (Or use a hand potato masher.) Add the milk, chives, butter, and salt and pepper to taste. Pulse just until somewhat smooth but still lumpy. Serve with the cutlets.

duck breast on mixed greens

2   *boneless duck breast halves, about 1½ pounds total, trimmed of all but a thin layer of fat and pounded evenly to about two-thirds of their original thickness (by the butcher if possible)*
    Salt and freshly ground black pepper
6   *ounces mesclun or other salad mix (about 6 cups)*
⅓   *cup raspberry vinegar*
⅓   *cup chicken stock*

1   Put a heavy skillet over medium heat. Season the duck with salt and pepper. (If the butcher hasn't done so, pound the duck between two sheets of aluminum foil or wax paper with the side of a cleaver or a meat pounder before seasoning.) Raise the heat under the skillet to high, add the duck, fat side down, and cook for 4 minutes. Turn and cook on the other side for 4 minutes for medium rare.

2   Meanwhile, put the salad mix in a salad spinner, fill with water, drain, and spin the greens dry. Remove any excess moisture with paper towels. Use the leaves whole or coarsely chop and evenly divide among three plates. Mix the raspberry vinegar and chicken stock in a cup.

3   Remove the duck to a cutting board. Add the vinegar and stock to the skillet over high heat and stir with a wooden spoon, scraping any bits from the bottom. Cook for 2 minutes to reduce the sauce slightly while you slice the duck thinly on the diagonal. Fan the duck slices on the salad greens. Spoon about 2 tablespoons of the sauce over each plate.

This dish looks as if it could have been prepared by a chef in a trendy restaurant instead of by you at home in fifteen minutes. You can also use boneless lamb steaks or chicken breasts instead of duck. Unlike chicken, duck can be served medium to medium rare, depending on your preference. Most supermarkets now have salad bar mixes labeled mesclun or gourmet salad mix. But even a packaged salad mix can work in a pinch for this recipe.

Serves 3

69

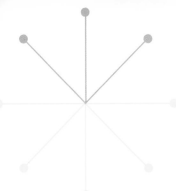

SEAFOOD

SEAFOOD is a dream come true for a hungry person in a hurry because it cooks so fast. In fact, seafood cooks faster than you might realize because so many people overcook it.

Fillets are the most convenient cut of fish for cooking because there are no heads, fins, or bones to worry about. Well, almost. Many fillets have annoying small bones called pin bones, which I prefer to remove before cooking. To locate these bones, rub your fingers over the fillet. Some people use needle-nose pliers to remove these bones. I often just pull them out with my fingers. The fish fillets used in the recipes in this chapter have had the bones removed before preparation begins. If you can get your fish-monger to do this, all the better.

Since freshness in fish is essential, make sure fillets have a bright clear look with uniform color and no gaps in the flesh. Obviously smell is a good indicator too. Fish—all seafood, really—should have a clean sea-breeze scent. That goes double for your fish store or the seafood section of your supermarket.

I prefer fillets to steaks when those steaks have a lot of bones, like salmon steaks. However, such steaks do hold up better in cooking, especially grilling. Other steaks, like swordfish and tuna, have no bones but get their name from their meaty appearance.

As with produce, you should buy whatever fish looks good that day, regardless of what the recipe you had in mind dictates. Better to change recipes than use an inferior piece of fish, especially at today's prices. Fortunately, in three of the four fish dishes in this chapter, you can make several substitutions.

The test for doneness in any cooked fish is a springy sensation when pressed with a finger. If the fish flakes when pressed, it's overdone. If the finger leaves an indentation, or the flesh is a bit squishy, the fish is underdone. The exceptions are meaty fish like salmon. Here there is some latitude depending on personal preference. For example, I don't like my salmon stone cold in the middle, like a rare steak. Rather, I like it closer to medium, with some darkness in the middle showing that the innermost part is not fully cooked. That is how the fish emerges in Asian-Spiced Salmon with Braised Bok Choy (page 75).

Shellfish fall into two camps. One includes mussels, clams, and other varieties that must be cleaned before they can be cooked. Even though they cook rather quickly, the cleaning takes too long for this book, so I don't use them. Other shellfish, like crab, shrimp, and scallops, are sold out of, as well as in, their shells. Squid is increasingly sold already cleaned. For Crab Cakes with Apple-Walnut Slaw (page 82), I use jumbo lump crab—large pieces of meat from the blue crab. While expensive, this crabmeat has almost no pieces of shell or cartilage. So, it saves time picking through the meat to find them. I figure that's worth the extra three dollars a pound.

The shrimp used in Shrimp and Goat Cheese Quesadilla with Avocado Salsa (page 80) and Jambalaya (page 87) in this chapter—and for recipes elsewhere in the book like Warm Shrimp and White Bean Salad with New Potatoes (page 144)—are already shelled. Again, they are a bit more expensive but worth the convenience. Not deveining shrimp also saves time. Cooked shrimp may seem like a godsend for fast meals, but I don't recommend them for hot dishes. In the reheating process, they're bound to go over the edge and become rubbery. They are fine for cold dishes.

Sea scallops are available year-round, and the smaller, more expensive bay scallops only in winter. I prefer sea scallops anyway, so my wallet and I are not usually disappointed. Most scallops come with a small strip (sometimes called a hinge) attached to one side of the muscle, like mini–adhesive bandages. I normally remove these before cooking.

As with most other dishes in this book, panfrying, sautéing, or steaming on top of the stove is the pre-ferred method for cooking seafood. You can also grill fish steaks or fillets on a gas-fired grill in fifteen minutes if the grill heats up quickly. While the grill heats (usually within ten minutes), the fish can soak in a marinade such as one made of olive oil, lemon juice, and garlic, or one of sesame oil, soy sauce, and rice wine. A microwave oven also does a decent job of cooking fish in a hurry. It's actually faster than the stovetop or grill, but doesn't give you the same flavor.

After frying, sautéing, grilling, and microwaving, simple stove-top stews are a good way to cook seafood quickly, as in Fifteen-Minute Bouillabaisse (page 84) and Jambalaya (page 87). These dishes give you a lot of leeway for substitutions, not only for the seafood but for the other ingredients. For example, by using all shellfish and adding some prosciutto, almonds, and a roasted red bell pepper, you can transform the French bouillabaisse into a Spanish zarzuela. Jambalaya has as many variations as there are Louisianans. Green bell peppers, oysters, and filé powder are but three ingredients you might consider adding or sub-stituting.

steamed cod with summer vegetables

This refreshing meal is perfect for warm summer evenings. The fish is light because it is steamed, not fried. The vegetables are crisp and plentiful. Feel free to substitute rockfish, sea bass, striped bass, tilefish, pollack, or scrod for the cod, and other seasonal vegetables such as sugar snap peas or bell peppers for the beans and squash.

Serves 4

3	tablespoons extra-virgin olive oil
6	scallions
1	medium to large tomato, 8 to 12 ounces
4	small yellow zucchini or other yellow summer squash, about 1 pound
12	ounces small green beans, preferably haricots verts
1	8-ounce bottle clam juice
	Salt and freshly ground black pepper
4	cod fillets, 5 to 6 ounces each, pin bones removed
10	basil leaves

1   Put 1 ½ tablespoons of the oil in a large, deep, heavy skillet over medium-high heat. Trim the scallions and coarsely chop the white part and 3 inches of the green. Add to the skillet and sauté for 2 minutes while you core and chop the tomato. Add the tomato to the skillet and cook while you trim and thinly slice the zucchini and trim the stem ends from the green beans.

2   Add the zucchini, beans, clam juice, and salt and pepper to taste to the skillet. (Easy on the salt; clam juice is very salty.) Raise the heat to high, stir, cover, and cook for 1 minute, or until the liquid starts to boil.

3   Meanwhile, season the cod with salt and pepper. Put the fish on top of the vegetables, cover, and cook for 4 minutes, or until the fish feels springy to the touch.

4   While the fish cooks, stack the basil leaves, then roll and cut crosswise into ribbons. Remove the cod to 4 soup plates. Stir half of the basil into the vegetables and spoon the vegetables around the fish. Pour the cooking liquid over the top. Sprinkle with the remaining basil and drizzle with the remaining 1 ½ tablespoons olive oil.

panfried snapper with tomato salsa and basmati rice

1	**cup basmati rice**
1	**teaspoon salt, plus more to taste**
1 ½	**tablespoons olive oil**
1 ½	**tablespoons unsalted butter**
4	**red snapper fillets, about 6 ounces each, pin bones removed**
	Freshly ground black pepper
⅓	**cup all–purpose flour**
1	**tablespoon sliced pickled jalapeño peppers or 1 fresh jalapeño pepper**
1	**small sweet onion such as Vidalia or mild red onion, about 4 ounces**
1	**pound ripe tomatoes**
10	**sprigs cilantro**

1 While the hot-water tap runs, put the rice in a 2-quart saucepan. Add 2 cups hot tap water and 1 teaspoon salt. Bring to a boil over high heat, then reduce the heat to low, cover and cook for 10 minutes. Turn off the heat and keep covered until ready to serve. (Or put the rice, 2 cups hot tap water, and 1 teaspoon salt in a 2-quart microwave-safe container. Cover and cook in a microwave oven on high power for 10 minutes. Keep covered until ready to serve.)

2 Meanwhile, put the oil and butter in a large, heavy skillet over medium-high heat. Season the fish with salt and pepper. Put the flour on a pie plate or wax paper. Dredge the fish in the flour, shaking off any excess. Add the fish to the skillet, skin side down, and cook for 4 minutes. Reduce heat to medium and cook for 4 minutes on the other side, or until the fish feels springy to the touch.

3 While the fish and rice cook, drop the jalapeño down the chute of a food processor with the motor of running. (If using a fresh jalapeño, stem and seed it first.) Stop the motor and scrape down the sides of the bowl with a rubber spatula. Peel and quarter the onion. Add to the processor and pulse a few times to chop very coarsely. Core and quarter the tomatoes. Remove the leaves from 6 of the cilantro sprigs. Add the tomato, cilantro, and salt and black pepper to taste to the processor. Pulse until the salsa is fully combined but still somewhat chunky.

4 Divide the fish and rice among four plates and garnish with the remaining cilantro sprigs. Spoon some of the salsa over the fish. Put the remaining salsa in a small bowl for the table.

Fish fillets for panfrying offer many more variations than meat or poultry. Almost any reasonably firm white-fleshed fish such as pollack, scrod, or sea bass can be substituted for the snapper in this dish. The amount of salsa is a little more than you may need, but it's a nice treat with tomorrow's tortilla chips. Or use it (well drained) in Shrimp and Goat Cheese Quesadilla with Avocado Salsa (page 80) instead of the tomato and cilantro.

Serves 4

asian-spiced salmon with braised bok choy

4	tablespoons peanut oil
4	salmon fillets, about 6 ounces each, pin bones removed
2	tablespoons Chinese five-spice powder
4	cloves garlic
2	medium stalks bok choy, about 1 ½ pounds
	Salt and freshly ground black pepper
¾	cup chicken stock

1   Put 2 tablespoons of the oil in a heavy skillet large enough to hold all the fillets in one layer without crowding. Put the skillet over medium-high heat. Rub the fillets with the five-spice powder. Put the salmon in the skillet, skin side down, cover, and cook for 3 minutes. Turn the fillets and cook for 3 minutes. Turn off the heat and let the salmon keep warm in the skillet.

2   While the salmon cooks, fill the sink with cold water. Put the remaining 2 tablespoons oil in a large, deep skillet, Dutch oven, or wok over medium-low heat. Peel the garlic. Drop the garlic down the chute of a food processor with the motor running. Scrape the garlic into the skillet and cook for 1 to 2 minutes, stirring once or twice to prevent burning.

3   While the garlic cooks, cut 1 inch from the bottoms of the bok choy and cut off any damaged tops from the leaves. Cut the leafy top half of the bok choy crosswise into 2-inch-wide strips and the thicker bottom half into 1-inch-wide strips. Wash briefly but vigorously in the sink and add to the skillet, without draining. Season with salt and pepper to taste, add the chicken stock, and stir. Raise the heat to high, cover, and cook for 4 to 5 minutes, or until the thickest parts of the stems are just tender.

4   To serve, put a salmon fillet in the center of a large soup plate with the bok choy on both sides. Spoon the cooking broth from the bok choy over the top of the bok choy.

When my sister Maria tried this dish she said, "This is one I'd gladly serve company." Spending more time with guests while still having a delicious meal, what a concept! The rich salmon marries well with the fragrant Chinese five-spice powder. Ditto for the hearty bok choy and garlic.

Serves 4

scallops and shiitake mushrooms with pea purée

This recipe was inspired by one that appears in Recipes 1-2-3 *by Rozanne Gold. Try it with a pinot blanc or somewhat dry riesling.*

Serves 3

1	**10–ounce package frozen baby peas (2 cups)**
3	**tablespoons unsalted butter**
4	**ounces shiitake mushrooms, preferably without stems**
1	**pound sea scallops**
½	**teaspoon herbes de Provence**
⅓	**cup dry vermouth or dry white wine**
	Salt and freshly ground black pepper
4	**chives**

1   While the hot-water tap runs, put the peas in a 1 ½ quart microwave-safe container. Add 3 tablespoons hot tap water, cover, and cook in a microwave oven on high power for 7 minutes. (Or put the peas and ⅓ cup hot water in a small saucepan, cover, and cook on the stovetop over medium-high heat for 6 minutes.)

2   Meanwhile, melt 1 ½ tablespoons of the butter in large, heavy skillet over medium-high heat. Remove and discard any stems from the mushrooms and thinly slice the caps. Remove the tough, small strip on the sides of the scallops. If necessary, cut the scallops to make them as close to uniform in size as possible.

3   Raise the heat under the skillet to high and add the scallops. Cook for 1 ½ minutes, turning once halfway through. Add the mushrooms and cook for 2 minutes. Add the herbes de Provence, vermouth, and salt and pepper to taste. Cook for 3 minutes while you coarsely chop the chives. The mushrooms will be just wilted and the scallops lightly browned.

4   Put the cooked peas and their liquid in a food processor with the remaining 1 ½ tablespoons of butter and salt and pepper to taste, and purée. To serve, ring a serving platter with the purée and put the scallops and mushrooms in the middle. Sprinkle with the chives.

san diego fish tacos

½	cup canola oil
1	cup beer
1	large egg
¾	cup all-purpose flour
½	teaspoon dry mustard
¼	teaspoon cayenne pepper
1	teaspoon salt
	Freshly ground black pepper
2	fillets white fish such as scrod, pollack, snapper, haddock, halibut, or catfish, 8 ounces each, pin bones removed and each fillet cut cross-wise into 6 pieces (by the fishmonger if possible)
1	small to medium sweet onion such as Vidalia, 4 to 8 ounces
10	sprigs cilantro
½	cup light or regular mayonnaise
½	cup low-fat yogurt
1	small head green cabbage, 12 to 16 ounces
2	ripe but firm avocados
1	lime
1	12-ounce jar medium-hot salsa
12	flour tortillas, about 8 inches in diameter

While visiting San Diego a number of years ago, I fell in love with fish tacos, that city's signature dish. Cabbage makes a crunchy and nutritious alternative to the iceberg lettuce normally used in tacos. Like most tacos, this one is a little messy to eat, so have plenty of napkins around.

Serves 4

1   Put the oil in a large, heavy skillet over medium-high heat. Combine the beer, egg, and flour in a medium-size mixing bowl. Stir in the mustard, cayenne, salt, and several grindings of black pepper. Put 6 pieces of fish in the batter, coat well, and add to the skillet. Cook for 3 minutes, turn the pieces, and cook for 3 more minutes, or until golden brown. Drain on a paper towel–lined platter. Repeat with the remaining 6 pieces. Reduce the heat if needed to prevent burning.

2   While the fish cooks, peel and quarter the onion and remove the leaves from the cilantro sprigs. Put the onion and cilantro in a food processor and pulse several times, or until coarsely chopped. Add the mayonnaise and yogurt to the processor and pulse just once or twice to combine. Put the onion-mayonnaise sauce in a small bowl.

CONTINUED

3   Halve the cabbage lengthwise and remove the core from each half. Place each half, flat side down, on a cutting surface and cut into thin shreds with a chef's knife. (Or shred using the large holes of a four-sided grater or the grating attachment of a food processor.) You should have about 4 cups. Put the cabbage in a small bowl.

4   Halve, pit, and peel the avocados. Cut each half lengthwise into six slices. Lay the slices on a small plate. Cut the lime into 4 wedges and put in a small dish. Put the salsa in a small bowl with a slotted spoon (so you won't get a lot of liquid in your tacos).

5   Bring all the ingredients for the tacos to the table and allow diners to make tacos one at a time as follows: Put a few tablespoons cabbage in the middle of each tortilla. Top with 1 piece of fish, 1 tablespoon of the onion-mayonnaise sauce, 1 tablespoon salsa, 2 avocado slices, and a squeeze of lime. Fold and eat.

shrimp and goat cheese quesadilla with avocado salsa

Most restaurant quesadillas are just a cheesy goo in between crisp tortillas. But this one has more flavor, texture, and substance than any restaurant quesadilla I've ever had. If you don't like shrimp, try crabmeat, chicken, and turkey, even left-over meats. Cheeses could be feta (with leftover lamb for a Middle Eastern touch), Cheddar (with leftover beef, perhaps), Monterey Jack, or Gouda.

Serves 4

2	tablespoons vegetable or olive oil
1	pound shelled raw shrimp
1	medium to large ripe tomato, 8 to 12 ounces
6	sprigs cilantro
2	flour tortillas, about 10 inches in diameter
8	ounces goat cheese
1-2	tablespoons sliced pickled jalapeño peppers or 1 to 2 fresh jalapeño peppers
	Salt and freshly ground black pepper
1	small to medium sweet onion such as Vidalia, about 8 ounces
2	ripe but firm avocados
1	lime

1 Put the oil in a large, heavy (preferably nonstick) skillet over medium-high heat. Cut each shrimp crosswise into 3 or 4 pieces. Add to the skillet, raise the heat to high, and cook for 2 minutes, stirring once or twice. Meanwhile, core, dice, and briefly drain the tomato in a sieve or small colander. Chop the leaves from the cilantro sprigs. Remove the shrimp to a plate and place 1 tortilla in the skillet. Reduce the heat to medium.

2 Spread the shrimp evenly on the tortilla, crumble the goat cheese on top, then spread the tomatoes and cilantro evenly over the shrimp and cheese. Finely chop the jalapeño slices and spread on top. (If using fresh jalapeños, stem and seed them first.) Season with salt and pepper to taste. Top with the second tortilla and cook for 3 minutes. Invert a plate the same diameter as the skillet over the quesadilla, then flip the quesadilla onto the plate, cooked side up. Slide the quesadilla back into the skillet, uncooked side down, and cook for 4 minutes.

3 Meanwhile, peel and quarter the onion. Put in a food processor and pulse a few times to chop very coarsely. Halve, pit, peel, and quarter the avocado. Juice the lime. Add the avocado, lime juice, and salt and pepper to taste to the processor. Pulse a few times, or until the salsa is fully combined but still a bit chunky. Cut the quesadilla into wedges—right in the pan or after putting it on a platter. Serve with the avocado salsa.

crab cakes with apple-walnut slaw

These crab cakes are fabulous, bursting with crab flavor and spiced with a healthy dose of cayenne pepper. The secret is using jumbo lump crabmeat, which has almost no shells. Lump crabmeat has a smattering of shells that must be picked out before using. If you can find a small head of cabbage, between twelve and sixteen ounces, it will be enough for this recipe. Otherwise buy a larger cabbage, use half, and save the rest for San Diego Fish Tacos (page 77).

Serves 4

¼	cup peanut or canola oil
1	pound jumbo lump crabmeat
6	saltine crackers
6	scallions
1	tablespoon Dijon mustard
½	cup mayonnaise
1	egg yolk
1	teaspoon cayenne pepper
	Salt and freshly ground black pepper
1	cup all-purpose flour
1	small head green cabbage, 12 to 16 ounces
1	small tart red apple
⅓	cup walnut pieces
1	tablespoon white vinegar
1	teaspoon sugar

1 Put the oil in a heavy skillet large enough to hold 4 crab cakes in one layer without crowding. Set the skillet over medium-low heat. Put the crabmeat in a large mixing bowl and crush the saltines over it. Trim the scallions and chop the white part and 1 inch of the green. Add the scallions, mustard, ¼ cup of the mayonnaise, egg yolk, cayenne, and salt and pepper to taste to the crab. Mix well.

2 Put the flour on a pie plate or wax paper. Form the crab mixture into 4 cakes. Raise the heat under the skillet to medium-high. Press the crab cakes into the flour to coat evenly and lightly pat off any excess. One by one, add the crab cakes to the skillet—the easiest way is to gently lower them into the skillet with a wide spatula. Cook for 4 minutes on each side, turning them with care, until golden brown and heated through. Reduce the heat if needed to prevent burning. Drain on a paper towel–lined platter.

3   While the crab cakes cook, halve the cabbage lengthwise and remove the core from each half. Place each half flat side down on a cutting surface and cut into thin shreds with a chef's knife. (Or shred using the large holes of a four-sided grater or the grating attachment of a food processor.) You should have about 4 cups. Put the cabbage in a large mixing bowl.

4   Core but do not peel the apple and cut into ⅜-inch cubes. If any walnut pieces are large, coarsely chop them. Add the apples and walnuts to the cabbage. In a small bowl, combine the remaining ¼ cup mayonnaise, vinegar, sugar, and salt and pepper to taste. Add the dressing to the cabbage and mix well. Put the crab cakes on individual plates and serve with the coleslaw.

fifteen-minute bouillabaisse

Most restaurants don't serve bouil-labaisse, and many that do serve it only on certain days of the week—for a pretty penny too. Now you can have bouil-labaisse any day of the week in fifteen minutes, and that includes the croûtes (toasted baguette slices) and the spicy mayonnaiselike rouille! A Provençal rosé would be a good accompaniment.

Serves 4

8	tablespoons extra-virgin olive oil
1	medium onion, about 8 ounces
4	cloves garlic
1	large tomato, about 12 ounces, or one 15-ounce can whole tomatoes
2	8-ounce bottles clam juice
2	teaspoons ground fennel
	Salt and freshly ground black pepper
½	teaspoon saffron threads
3	pieces monkfish or swordfish, about 4 ounces each
3	pieces halibut, snapper, or sea bass, about 4 ounces each
8	ounces cleaned squid bodies
1	small French baguette
½	cup roasted red bell peppers from a jar
1	egg yolk (see Note)

1   Preheat a broiler and adjust the broiling rack so it is 3 to 6 inches from the heat source. Put 1 tablespoon of the oil in a large, deep, heavy skillet over medium-high heat. Peel and quarter the onion. Peel the garlic. Put the onion and 3 cloves of the garlic in a food processor. Pulse just until chopped. Scrape into the skillet, raise the heat to high, and cook for 2 minutes. Meanwhile, core the tomato, put it in the food processor, and pulse until chopped. (If using canned tomatoes, drain the tomatoes and coarsely chop.) Open the bottles of clam juice.

2   Add the tomato, clam juice, fennel, and salt and pepper to taste to the skillet. Over the skillet, crush ¼ teaspoon of the saffron between your fingers. Stir well, cover, and bring to a boil. Meanwhile, cut each piece of fish in half. Reduce the heat under the skillet to medium, add the fish, cover, and cook for 5 minutes. Meanwhile, cut the squid into rings. Add the squid for the final 1 minute.

3   While the seafood cooks, cut the baguette on the diagonal into nine ½-inch slices. Put 8 of the slices on a baking sheet and toast both sides in the broiler, about 1 minute on each side.

CONTINUED

fifteen-minute bouillabaisse

4   Drop the remaining garlic clove down the chute of the food processor with the motor running. Stop the motor and scrape down the sides of the bowl with a rubber spatula. Add the roasted peppers, egg yolk, reserved bread slice, and remaining ¼ teaspoon saffron, crushed between your fingers. Purée, then, with the motor running, gradually add the remaining 7 tablespoons olive oil through the chute until the mixture has the consistency of mayonnaise. Season to taste with salt.

5   Divide the seafood and broth among 4 soup plates. Spread the rouille on the toasted baguette slices and put 2 slices on top of each plate. Serve any remaining rouille in a small bowl at the table.

Note: If you have concerns about using raw eggs, replace the egg in this recipe with ¼ cup egg substitute.

jambalaya

1	cup basmati rice
1	teaspoon salt, plus more to taste
1½	tablespoons canola or vegetable oil
3	cloves garlic
1	medium onion, about 8 ounces
2	medium ribs celery
1	8-ounce can tomato sauce
1	tablespoon fresh thyme leaves or 1 teaspoon dried thyme
3	cups chicken stock or 2 cups clam juice and 1 cup water
3	bay leaves
1	teaspoon Tabasco or other hot-pepper sauce, or to taste
8	ounces kielbasa or other cooked spicy sausage
1	pound shelled raw shrimp
6	chives

You'll make Paul Prudhomme proud— and perhaps a bit envious—with this fifteen-minute version of a Creole classic. Serve it with lots of crusty French bread for dunking.

Serves 4

1   While the hot-water tap runs, put the rice in a 2-quart saucepan. Add 2 cups hot tap water and 1 teaspoon salt. Bring to a boil over high heat, then reduce the heat to low, cover and cook for 10 minutes. (Or put the rice, 2 cups hot water, and 1 teaspoon salt in a 2-quart microwave-safe container. Cover and cook in a microwave oven on high power for 10 minutes.)

2   Meanwhile, put the oil in a large, deep, heavy skillet over medium-high heat. Peel the garlic. Peel and quarter the onion. Trim and quarter the celery. Put the garlic, onion, and celery in a food processor. Pulse just until chopped. Scrape into the skillet, raise the heat to high, and cook for 2 minutes, stirring once or twice.

3   While the vegetables cook, open the can of tomato sauce and chop the thyme leaves. (If using dried thyme, crush with your fingers.) Add the tomato sauce, thyme, stock, bay leaves, and Tabasco to the skillet, cover, and bring to a boil. Meanwhile, cut the sausage into ¼-inch-thick rounds. Add the sausage, stir well, cover, and cook for 3 minutes.

4   Add the shrimp, stir well, cover, and cook for 2 minutes. Meanwhile, chop the chives. Add the cooked rice to the skillet, stir, cover, and bring to a boil. Turn off the heat and taste for seasoning. Serve in soup plates sprinkled with the chives.

PASTA & GRAINS

WHENEVER I can't think of what to eat or if the cupboard is lean, pasta invariably comes to mind. Almost anything can go on or with pasta. Usually I just open the fridge or look in the pantry and see what's available. That's why I often call my impromptu pasta meals "throw togethers." The pasta sauce could contain canned chickpeas and roasted red bell peppers from a jar; feta cheese, kalamata olives, and oregano; cooked sausage and frozen peas; canned cannellini beans and olive oil–packed tuna; and on and on. To say pasta combinations are endless is redundancy in the extreme.

Although pasta takes very little time to cook, most people need more than fifteen minutes. Pasta dishes can be had in under fifteen minutes by following three tips. The first is to start with hot tap water. Some people don't like to cook with hot water from the tap because they are unsure of the quality of the water. If you prefer to use water from the cold tap, you'll need to add a few minutes to the cooking times of the recipes in this chapter.

Next, divide the water into two pots, one of which should be large enough to hold all the water when the contents of the two pots are combined. The larger pot should have a capacity of eight quarts. When you use two pots, the pasta water comes to a boil much faster, in less than ten minutes. A larger pot helps to avoid boiling over, something you don't want to be concerned about when you're scurrying around making the sauce. Normally four quarts of water are used to cook a pound of pasta, but I've found that three quarts will work with fresh pasta or thin dried pasta like capellini. However, it is important to give the pasta a vigorous stir when it first goes into the pot and again when the water returns to a boil. When I add vegetables to the pot, as in Pasta with Asparagus, Prosciutto, and Parmesan (page 91), I use four quarts of water.

The third key to making pasta dishes in less than a quarter of an hour is the pasta itself. Capellini is the only dried pasta I use because it cooks in four minutes or less once the water comes to a boil. Other dried pastas take anywhere from a few minutes to ten minutes longer. If you want to use another type of dried pasta, you won't be able to make the dish in fifteen minutes. However, there are an increasing variety of fresh pastas that cook as fast as or faster than dried capellini.

Dried pasta is cooked until it is al dente, or firm to the bite. For softer pasta, add a minute or so to the cooking time. Fresh pasta, by its very nature, can't achieve the same firm consistency of dried pasta.

While a pasta pot with a built-in colander is convenient, it isn't essential. In fact, I never owned one until very recently. Having a pasta pot with a built-in colander enables you to drain the pasta right over the pot. The pasta can then be transferred to a nearby mixing bowl, skillet, or wok. A built-in colander also makes it easier to add pasta cooking water to create a sauce.

An alternative is to drain the pasta into a normal colander set in a large mixing bowl in the sink. Using a traditional colander actually has an advantage over pots with built-in colanders because the drained pasta pot becomes a perfect container for mixing the cooked pasta with the sauce.

All pasta dishes call for cheese that is already grated. Grated cheese keeps reasonably well in the freezer and needs no defrosting before use.

Almost all couscous sold in the United States is precooked. This enables it to cook in a fraction of the time of traditional couscous, making it perfect for Couscous with Mergez Sausage (page 100). Though it is technically a pasta, most people think of couscous as a separate grain. Yet this versatile ingredient can be used like pasta or like rice in hot and cold preparations, for main dishes and for side dishes. Use the basic method for Couscous with Mergez Sausage to prepare as many different dishes as you might with conventional pasta. While the couscous steams in a bowl, prepare the other ingredients.

Beans, especially chickpeas, are good with couscous. Lamb goes well with it, and so do chicken and shrimp. Seasonings could follow the spice route of North Africa, where couscous is a staple. A couscous dish could have Italian, Spanish, or Greek touches as well, with an assortment of olives, roasted red bell peppers, and a variety of cheeses, especially goat cheeses. Cilantro is the herb I most associate with couscous. Mint is also very appropriate.

I use quick-cooking brown rice in Seafood Pilaf with Saffron and Peas (page 98) because it cooks much faster than normal brown rice, even faster than long-grain white rice. As an alternative, you may want to try other quick-cooking rice, or basmati rice, which I use in all other dishes that call for rice.

Warm Tabbouleh with Feta, Chickpeas, and Mint (page 99) may seem odd to those used to cold tabbouleh, and one with far more parsley than mine. But hot bulgur dishes, usually in the form of pilafs, are quite common in the eastern Mediterranean, especially Turkey. Besides, cold tabbouleh takes too long.

pasta with asparagus, prosciutto, and parmesan

1	**pound asparagus spears of medium thickness**
1	**tablespoon salt, plus more to taste**
1	**pound dried capellini or fresh pasta of any kind**
6	**ounces sliced prosciutto**
3	**tablespoons extra–virgin olive oil**
	Grated nutmeg
	Freshly ground black pepper
1/3	**cup grated Parmesan cheese, plus cheese at the table**

1   Run the hot-water tap and put 2 quarts hot tap water in each of 2 pots (one large enough to eventually hold all the water, pasta, and asparagus). Cover and bring both pots to a boil over high heat, 8 to 10 minutes. Meanwhile, cut the bottom 1 inch from the asparagus spears and discard. Cut the spears on the diagonal into 1½-inch pieces.

2   When the water boils, transfer the water from the smaller pot into the larger pot. Add the 1 tablespoon salt, pasta, and asparagus. Stir, cover, and return to a boil. Stir again, partially cover, and cook for 3 to 4 minutes, or until the pasta is done to your taste. (The asparagus will be cooked but firm.)

3   While the pasta and asparagus cook, cut the prosciutto slices crosswise into ½-inch-wide strips. Combine the olive oil, nutmeg, and salt, and pepper to taste in a cup. Drain the pasta and asparagus, reserving ½ cup of the cooking liquid. Put the pasta and asparagus back into the pasta pot. Add the prosciutto and the olive oil mixture and toss well. Add the cheese and cooking water and toss well. Serve in soup plates or pasta bowls. Pass the additional cheese at the table.

The trifecta of asparagus, prosciutto, and Parmesan is a natural for pasta, especially in spring when local fresh asparagus is in full swing. Have the prosciutto sliced a bit thicker than normal so it can more easily be cut into strips.

Serves 4

penne with broccoli, garlic, and pecorino

Garlic and anchovies are great flavor enhancers in any pantry, even for people who don't particularly like anchovies. When cooked, the anchovies mellow like garlic. Try this dish with an Italian barbera or dolcetto.

Serves 4

1	**head broccoli, about 1¼ pounds**
1	**tablespoon salt, plus more to taste**
1	**pound fresh penne or other fresh short pasta**
3	**tablespoons extra-virgin olive oil**
6	**cloves garlic**
3	**anchovy fillets**
½	**teaspoon hot-pepper flakes, plus flakes for the table**
½	**cup grated pecorino cheese, plus cheese for the table**

1 Run the hot-water tap and put 2 quarts hot tap water in each of 2 pots (one large enough to eventually hold all the water, pasta, and broccoli). Cover and bring both pots to a boil over high heat, 8 to 10 minutes. Meanwhile, cut the bottom 1 inch from the broccoli stems. Separate the stems from the heads. Peel the stems and cut crosswise into ¼-inch-thick slices. Separate the heads into florets. Rinse in a colander large enough to hold the cooked pasta.

2 When the water boils, transfer the water from the smaller pot into the larger pot. Add the 1 tablespoon salt, pasta, and broccoli. Stir, cover, and return to a boil. Stir again, partially cover, and cook for 5 minutes, or until the pasta is done to your taste. (The broccoli will be cooked but firm.)

3 While the pasta and broccoli cook, put the oil in a wok or large skillet over medium heat. Peel the garlic. Drop the garlic down the chute of a food processor with the motor running. Add the anchovies and purée. Reduce the heat under the wok to medium-low and scrape the garlic-anchovy mixture into the wok. Cook for 2 minutes, add the hot pepper flakes, stir, and turn off the heat.

4 Drain the pasta and broccoli, reserving ½ cup of the cooking water. Add the pasta, broccoli, and cooking water to the wok with the garlic and anchovies. Toss well. Add the cheese and toss again. Taste and adjust for salt and hot pepper. Serve in soup plates or pasta bowls. Pass the additional cheese and hot-pepper flakes at the table.

spaghetti carbonara

1	**tablespoon olive oil**
6	**ounces pancetta or bacon**
3	**cloves garlic**
3	**large eggs**
½	**cup grated Parmesan cheese, plus more for the table**
⅓	**cup half-and-half**
1	**tablespoon salt, plus more to taste**
	Freshly ground black pepper
	Ground nutmeg
1	**pound fresh spaghetti or dried capellini**
5	**sprigs parsley, preferably flat-leaf**

1 Run the hot-water tap and put 1½ quarts hot tap water in each of 2 pots (one large enough to eventually hold all the water and pasta). Cover and bring both pots to a boil over high heat, 7 to 9 minutes.

2 Meanwhile, put the oil in a wok or large skillet over medium-high heat. Coarsely chop the pancetta, add to the wok and cook for 4 to 5 minutes, until crisp. While the pancetta cooks, peel and chop the garlic. Add the garlic, reduce the heat to medium-low, and cook for 2 minutes, then turn off the heat. (Be careful not to let the garlic burn.) Beat the eggs, cheese, half-and-half, and salt, pepper, and nutmeg to taste in a bowl.

3 When the water boils, transfer the water from the smaller pot into the larger pot. Add the 1 tablespoon salt and the pasta. Stir, cover, and return to a boil. Stir again, partially cover, and cook for 3 to 4 minutes, or until the pasta is done to your taste. Meanwhile, chop the parsley.

4 When the pasta is cooked, drain, reserving 1 cup of the cooking water. Add the pasta to the pancetta mixture in the wok over low heat. Add the egg mixture and mix well. Add the cooking water, ⅓ cup at a time, until the pasta is well coated. Serve in soup plates or pasta bowls. Sprinkle with parsley and additional pepper. Pass the additional cheese at the table.

This is the kind of dish you can usually make in a pinch because the ingredients are almost always around, especially if you make it in the more austere, classic fashion, without garlic, nutmeg, or parsley. Though pancetta—Italian unsmoked bacon, sold in pinwheel rounds in better butcher shops and delis—is traditionally used, regular bacon is fine. Prosciutto can also be used for a lower-fat version.

Serves 4

spaghetti bolognese

I can remember taking an hour or more to make this rich and flavorful sauce when I was the chef of an Italian restaurant in Philadelphia. Like the classic Bolognese sauce, this one has chicken livers. If someone in your family can't handle them, feel free to leave them out.

Serves 4

8	ounces sweet Italian sausage, preferably without casings
8	ounces lean ground beef
4	ounces chicken livers
1	small onion, about 4 ounces
1	rib celery
2	15-ounce cans tomato sauce
1/4	cup dry white wine
1	tablespoon salt plus more to taste
1	pound fresh spaghetti or fettuccine or dried capellini
1/3	cup heavy cream
1/2 – 3/4	teaspoon ground nutmeg
	Freshly ground black pepper
	Grated Parmesan cheese for the table

1 Run the hot-water tap and put 1½ quarts hot tap water in each of 2 pots (one large enough to eventually hold all the water and pasta). Cover and bring both pots to a boil over high heat, 7 to 9 minutes.

2 Meanwhile, put a large, deep, heavy skillet over high heat. Remove the casings from the sausage, if there are any, and briefly crumble the sausage and beef together in a mixing bowl. Add the sausage and beef to the skillet and cook while you pat dry and cut the chicken livers into ½-inch pieces. Add to the skillet and cook for 3 minutes, breaking up any large clumps of meat, until the meat loses its red color.

3 While the meat cooks, peel and quarter the onion. Trim the celery and cut into 4 cross-wise pieces. Put the onion and celery in a food processor and pulse several times until just chopped. Add vegetables to the skillet and cook for 2 minutes, stirring, while you open the cans of tomato sauce. Add the tomato sauce and wine to the skillet, cover, and bring to a boil, stirring once or twice.

4 When the water boils, transfer the water from the smaller pot into the larger pot. Add the 1 tablespoon salt and the pasta. Stir, cover, and return to a boil. Stir again, partially cover, and cook for 3 to 4 minutes, or until the pasta is done to your taste.

5   Meanwhile, add the cream, nutmeg, and salt and pepper to taste to the skillet. Bring to a simmer (do not boil once the cream is added), stirring periodically, and cook until the pasta is done. Taste and adjust for salt and nutmeg. When the pasta is cooked, drain and divide among individual soup plates or pasta bowls. Top with the sauce. Pass the cheese at the table.

linguine with clams, parsley, and garlic

If I had to pick a favorite quick pasta, or any quick meal, this would be it. Garlic, pasta, and clams are a great flavor combination, and I always have them, as well as parsley, on hand. Canned clams are a decent substitute for fresh. No cheese is needed.

Serves 4

5	cloves garlic
10	sprigs parsley, preferably flat-leaf
2	tablespoons extra-virgin olive oil
½	cup white wine
½	cup bottled clam juice
3	6½-ounce cans chopped clams
½	teaspoon hot-pepper flakes
1	tablespoon salt, plus more to taste
1	pound fresh linguine or spaghetti or dried capellini
2	tablespoons unsalted butter

1 Run the hot-water tap and put 1 ½ quarts hot tap water in each of 2 pots (one large enough to eventually hold all the water and pasta). Cover and bring both pots to a boil over high heat, 7 to 9 minutes.

2 Meanwhile, peel the garlic. Drop the garlic down the chute a food processor with the motor running. Purée, then stop the motor and scrape down the sides of the bowl with a rubber spatula. Add the leaves from the parsley sprigs and pulse just until the leaves are chopped.

3 Put the oil in a wok or large skillet over high heat. Add the parsley-garlic mixture, reduce the heat to medium, and cook for 1 minute while you put the wine and clam juice in the bowl of the processor. Swirl to pick up any remaining garlic and parsley and add to the skillet. Raise the heat to high and cook for 2 minutes while you open the cans of clams. Add the clams and their juice and the hot-pepper flakes to the skillet. Cook for 3 minutes.

4 When the water boils, transfer the water from the smaller pot into the larger pot. Add the salt and pasta. Stir, cover, and return to a boil. Stir again, partially cover, and cook for 3 to 4 minutes, or until the pasta is done to your taste. Meanwhile, cut the butter into pieces.

5 When the pasta is cooked, drain and add to the wok with the clam mixture. Add the butter, reduce the heat to medium, and toss for 1 to 2 minutes, until the pasta is well coated with the sauce. Serve in soup plates or pasta bowls.

capellini with smoked salmon and scallion cream cheese

3	**scallions**
½	**cup whipped cream cheese**
⅓	**cup half-and-half**
	Freshly ground black pepper
1	**tablespoon salt, plus more to taste**
1	**pound dried capellini or fresh spaghetti**
8	**ounces smoked salmon**

1   Run the hot-water tap and put 1 ½ quarts hot tap water in each of 2 pots (one large enough to eventually hold all the water and pasta). Cover and bring both pots to a boil over high heat, 7 to 9 minutes.

2   Meanwhile, trim the scallions and remove all but the top 2 inches of the green parts. Reserve the tops and quarter the rest of the scallions crosswise. Put in a food processor and pulse until coarsely chopped. Add the cream cheese and pulse a few times just to incorporate. Pour the half-and-half through the chute with the motor of the processor running and purée until smooth. Season liberally with pepper.

3   When the water boils, transfer the water from the smaller pot into the larger pot. Add the 1 tablespoon salt and the pasta. Stir, cover, and return to a boil. Stir again, partially cover, and cook for 3 to 4 minutes, or until the pasta is done to your taste. Meanwhile, halve the scallion greens lengthwise, then thinly slice crosswise. Coarsely chop the salmon.

4   When the pasta is cooked, drain and reserve ½ cup of the cooking water. Put the pasta back into the cooking pot and toss with the salmon. Add the cooking water to the cream cheese with the motor of the processor running to create a thin creamy sauce. Pour the sauce over the pasta and toss well. Add salt to taste and toss. Serve in soup plates or pasta bowls. Sprinkle with additional pepper and the scallion greens.

Smoked salmon is a great resource for quick meals because it packs so much flavor. Some markets or delis sell salmon bits, odds and ends that are perfect for this dish, and at half the price of sliced salmon. If you want to make this dish a little special for company, sprinkle the finished pasta with some red salmon caviar or black sturgeon caviar.

Serves 4

seafood pilaf with saffron and peas

3	**cups chicken stock, bottled clam juice, or seafood stock**
¼	**teaspoon saffron threads**
4	**tablespoons olive oil**
1	**small onion, about 4 ounces**
1½	**cups quick-cooking brown rice or basmati rice**
1	**cup frozen baby peas**
6	**ounces shelled small raw shrimp**
6	**ounces bay or sea scallops**
8	**ounces cleaned squid bodies**
	Salt and freshly ground black pepper
	Cayenne pepper

Though pilafs, like risottos, are not often thought of as main dishes, they can easily become main dishes by incorporating meat, seafood, and legumes. Pilafs cook more quickly than risottos and don't require constant stirring. I make this particular pilaf with one of the many types of rice (not all quick cooking) from the Lundberg Family Farm in California. It's available at natural-food stores and better markets, though you could use any good quick-cooking rice or basmati rice.

Serves 4

1 Put the stock in a saucepan over high heat. Crush the saffron threads with your fingers into the stock, cover, and bring to a boil. Meanwhile, put 2 tablespoons of the oil in a large, heavy saucepan over medium-high heat. Halve the onion lengthwise, peel, and coarsely chop in a food processor. Add to the saucepan, raise the heat to high, stir, and cook for 1 minute. Add the rice, stir, and add the hot stock. Cover and cook for 8 minutes, reducing the heat to medium when the rice comes to a boil. (It should simmer briskly.)

2 While the rice cooks, run the hot-water tap and put the peas in a small colander under the hot running water for 1 minute to defrost them. Drain.

3 While the peas defrost, put the remaining 2 tablespoons oil in a large skillet over medium heat. Halve the shrimp crosswise, and halve the scallops if large. Raise the heat under the skillet to high, add the shrimp and scallops, and cook for 1 minute while you cut the squid crosswise into ⅜-inch-wide rings. Add the squid to the skillet and cook for 1 minute. Stir and season with salt, black pepper, and cayenne to taste.

4 Add the seafood and peas to the rice after the rice has cooked for about 8 minutes. Cover and cook for about 2 minutes, or until the rice has almost completely absorbed the stock—it should be slightly soupy and pleasantly chewy. Taste and adjust for salt, black pepper, and cayenne. Serve in soup plates.

warm tabbouleh with feta and chickpeas

1	cup medium-grain bulgur
	Salt
6	scallions
2	Kirby or small pickling cucumbers
1	medium to large ripe tomato, 8 to 12 ounces
²/₃	cup packed fresh mint leaves
²/₃	cup packed fresh parsley leaves, preferably flat-leaf
¹/₂	lemon
¹/₄	cup extra-virgin olive oil
	Cayenne pepper
	Freshly ground black pepper
1	15-ounce can chickpeas
8	ounces feta cheese

1   While the hot-water tap runs, put the bulgur and a healthy pinch of salt in a 2-quart microwave-safe container. Add 1 cup plus 2 tablespoons hot tap water, cover, and cook in a microwave oven on high power for 5 minutes. Let stand, covered, for 8 minutes. (Or put the bulgur, a healthy pinch of salt, and 1 cup plus 2 tablespoons hot water in a heavy 2-quart saucepan. Cook for 5 minutes over high heat, reducing the heat to low when the bulgur comes to a boil. Let stand, covered, for 8 minutes.)

2   Meanwhile, trim the scallions and remove all but 2 inches of the green part. Halve the scallions crosswise and put them in a food processor. Trim and quarter the cucumbers (but don't peel) and add to the processor. Pulse until very coarsely chopped. Cut the tomato in half lengthwise, gently squeeze out some of the juice and seeds, and cut each half into quarters. Add to the processor along with the mint and parsley. Pulse until coarsely chopped. Transfer the vegetables to a large serving bowl.

3   Juice the half lemon. Mix the lemon juice, oil, and cayenne, black pepper, and salt to taste in a cup. (Feta cheese is salty so go easy on the salt initially.) Open the can of chickpeas into a colander, rinse, drain briefly, and pat dry with paper towels. Put the chickpeas in the bowl with the vegetables.

4   Add the dressing and toss well. Crumble or coarsely chop the feta. Gently fold into the vegetables, then mix in the bulgur. Serve warm.

Classic tabbouleh is a cold salad that contains more parsley than bulgur. I prefer more of a bulgur flavor so I cut back on the parsley and use a medium-grain bulgur instead of the more traditional fine grain. This version is also bulked up for a main course with chickpeas and feta, which retain the Middle Eastern feel.

Serves 4

couscous with mergez sausage

I got to appreciate the rich and exotic cooking of Morocco when I visited that country several years ago. The cuisine is amazingly varied, but it doesn't have to be complicated, as this recipe shows. Mergez is a thin, spicy North African lamb sausage available in specialty and butcher shops and by mail (page 150). Other spicy sausage such as chorizo, hot Italian sausage, or spiced poultry sausage can be substituted.

Serves 4

1¼	cups instant couscous
1½	pounds mergez or other spicy sausage
5	scallions
1	medium to large ripe tomato, 8 to 12 ounces
1	4-ounce jar whole pimientos or roasted red bell peppers
20	oil-cured black olives, preferably pitted
⅓	cup packed fresh mint leaves
2	teaspoons ground cumin
	Salt
	Cayenne pepper

1 Run the hot-water tap and put 3 cups hot tap water in a 2-quart saucepan over high heat. Cover and bring to a boil. Add the couscous, stir, and reduce the heat to medium. Cook, uncovered, for 4 minutes, stirring once or twice. Turn off the heat, cover, and let the couscous steam for 6 minutes. (Or put the couscous and 2 cups hot water in a microwave-safe container and cook on high power for 4 minutes, then let the couscous steam for 6 minutes.)

2 Meanwhile, put a large, heavy skillet over high heat. Cut the sausage into 4-inch pieces. Add the sausage to the skillet, cover, and cook for 3 minutes. Turn once and cook for 4 minutes.

3 While the sausage cooks, trim the scallions and remove all but 1 inch of the green part. Halve the scallions crosswise, put them in a food processor, and pulse until coarsely chopped. Core and quarter the tomato. Quarter the pimientos. Pit the olives unless already pitted. Put the tomato, pimientos, olives, and mint leaves in the processor with the scallions and pulse several times until coarsely chopped and combined.

4 Put the steamed couscous in a mixing bowl and add the scallion mixture, cumin, and salt and cayenne to taste. Mix and fluff with a large fork. Transfer the couscous to the center of a serving platter and place the sausage around the edges.

EGGS

AFTER pasta, egg dishes are what my wife and I most frequently eat for dinner when nothing else seems to be in the house, or when leftovers are begging to be used up. Eggs provide solid protein, so they can easily be the focus of a main course. And because they go with so many foods, from smoked fish to fresh herbs to vegetables of almost every persuasion, you'll rarely tire of them.

Perhaps because eggs are associated with breakfast or brunch, they are seldom considered dinner fare. I've even seen some quick-recipe cookbooks that have no egg dishes at all. Yet eggs are among the great convenience foods for dinner precisely because they cook quickly.

Scrambled eggs are about as quick as it gets. The seasoning could be as simple as fresh parsley, salt, and pepper. But it could also include smoked salmon and fresh dill; roasted peppers and olives; or goat cheese and fresh thyme. I prefer omelets, particularly the two types of omelets in this chapter: the Italian frittata and the Spanish tortilla. The latter should not confused with Mexican flatbread. Unlike French omelets, which need to be folded, the frittata and the tortilla are served flat and thus require less manipulating. Both can be served in the pan, which I actually prefer. I like the way the omelet looks against the backdrop of my shiny black cast-iron skillet.

Both the frittata and the tortilla can be beefed up with everything from vegetables and cheese, as in Frittata with Artichoke Hearts, Roasted Peppers, and Pecorino (page 104) to beans and sausage, as in Spanish Tortilla with Baby Lima Beans and Potatoes (page 106). These omelets are great ways to get rid of leftovers too, whether the parslied potatoes and steamed broccoli from last night or that Cheddar cheese you just discovered in the back of the refrigerator. Come to think of it, those three leftovers together would make a great frittata or tortilla.

While Joe's Special with Shiitake Mushrooms (page 107) may seem like a scrambled egg dish, I think of it more as a kitchen-sink dish in which eggs are just one of the many ingredients thrown in. This San

Francisco specialty, like many signature dishes, was created out of necessity, so you shouldn't feel bad about making changes like using sausage meat instead of ground sirloin. The shiitake mushrooms are my personal twist.

I've rarely liked huevos rancheros in restaurants. They're usually covered with too much sauce or cheese, a common Tex-Mex restaurant problem. My Huevos Rancheros with Spicy Black Beans (page 108) is different. It's cleaner and fresher tasting but still quite satisfying.

This style of cooking eggs lends itself to many variations. For example, you could cook the black beans in a skillet with Mexican seasonings, put the eggs on top, cover, and let the eggs steam until done. Then you could top the dish with salsa. Or you could do what some might call eggs Florentine, by putting fried eggs on a bed of spinach.

Although eggs have gotten a bum rap for their fat and cholesterol, two eggs have only ten grams of fat, less than four ounces of skinless dark-meat chicken. If you're concerned about fat, you can poach eggs instead of frying them. Substituting a few egg whites for one or two of the yolks is another possibility for reducing fat, as is using egg substitutes.

frittata with artichokes, roasted peppers, and pecorino

1	**tablespoon olive oil or unsalted butter**
8	**large eggs**
¼	**cup milk**
1	**teaspoon crushed dried Greek or Sicilian oregano leaves or ground fennel**
	Salt and freshly ground black pepper
½	**small sweet onion such as a Vidalia, about 4 ounces**
1	**4-ounce jar whole pimientos or roasted red bell peppers**
3-4	**canned artichoke hearts packed in water**
4-5	**sprigs parsley, preferably flat-leaf**
⅓	**cup grated pecorino cheese**

1   Put the oil or butter in a 9- or 10-inch ovenproof skillet (cast iron is ideal) over medium-high heat. Beat the eggs with the milk, oregano, salt, and pepper in a mixing bowl. Add to the skillet and reduce the heat to medium-low. Turn on the broiler and adjust the broiler pan so it is 6 inches from the heat source.

2   Meanwhile, peel and quarter the onion half. Put in a food processor and pulse until chopped. You should have about ½ cup. Put the onion in the mixing bowl used to beat the eggs. Put the pimientos in the food processor and pulse until chopped. Add to the onion. Cut the artichokes into quarters (if they are small) or sixths (if they are large). Add to the onion and pepper. Chop the leaves from the parsley sprigs and add to the onion mixture. Mix well.

3   Gently add the onion mixture to the egg mixture in the skillet and spread it out evenly. Increase the heat to medium and cook for six minutes. When the bottom and sides of the frittata are set—the center will still be a little runny—sprinkle the pecorino evenly over the top.

4   Put the skillet in the broiler and cook for about 3 minutes, until the top is just firm and nicely browned. Turn the skillet a few times so the frittata browns evenly. If the top is well browned but the center is not yet firm, put the skillet on top of the stove over medium heat for 1 to 2 minutes. Cut the frittata into wedges and serve from the skillet.

Mom made this kind of omelet on meatless Fridays and all through Lent, though we never called them frittatas. But don't think of them as a sacrifice; frittatas are delicious year-round. When possible, I eat them at room temperature. Leftovers are great for the next day's breakfast or lunch. I like the flavor of dried Greek or Sicilian oregano. If you can't find them, use ground fennel, not the sharp-tasting "pizza" oregano.

Serves 4

spanish tortilla with baby lima beans and potatoes

While the Italians usually stick with vegetables inside their frittatas, Spanish tortilla fillings tend to be heartier, like this one, a favorite at our house. Normally, a tortilla is flipped over after cooking halfway through, a tricky proposition for most people, especially when they're in a rush. So I've modified my tortilla to cook like a frittata. Try this tortilla with a glass of bone-dry fino sherry.

Serves 4

3	tablespoons olive oil
1	medium red-skinned potato, about 8 ounces
1	medium onion, about 8 ounces
1	cup (half of a 10-ounce box) frozen baby lima beans or frozen peas
4	sprigs parsley, preferably flat-leaf
8	large eggs
	Salt and freshly ground black pepper
8	ounces cooked spicy sausage such as chorizo or kielbasa

1 Turn on the broiler and adjust the broiler pan so it is 6 inches from the heat source. Put the oil in a 9- or 10-inch ovenproof skillet (cast iron is ideal) over medium-high heat. Cut the potato in half lengthwise, then cut each half into 3 pieces. (No need to peel.) Put the pieces in a food processor and pulse about 20 times until the potato is diced. Add to the skillet, stir, cover, and cook for 3 minutes.

2 Meanwhile, peel and quarter the onion. Put in the food processor and pulse until chopped. Run the hot-water tap and put the lima beans in a 1-quart microwave-safe container. Add ¼ cup hot tap water, cover, and cook in a microwave oven on high power for 5 minutes. (Or put in a saucepan with 1 cup hot tap water, cover, and cook on the stovetop over high heat for 7 minutes.) Peas will take about half the time. Drain. While the lima beans cook, add the onion to the skillet and cook, stirring periodically, for about 3 minutes, or until the potatoes are barely cooked and the onions are lightly browned. Reduce the heat to medium.

3 Chop the leaves from the parsley sprigs. Beat the eggs, parsley, and salt and pepper to taste on a mixing bowl. Add to the skillet, spreading evenly. Cut the sausage into ½-inch or smaller cubes. Mix with the lima beans and salt to taste. Evenly spread this mixture over the eggs in the skillet. Cook for 3 to 4 minutes, or until the bottom and sides of the tortilla are set. The center will still be a little runny.

4 Put the skillet in the broiler and cook for about 3 minutes, or until the top is just firm and nicely browned. Turn the skillet a few times so the tortilla browns evenly. If the top is well browned but the center is not yet firm, put the skillet on top of the stove over medium heat for 1 to 2 minutes. Cut the tortilla into wedges. Serve from the skillet.

joe's special with shiitake mushrooms

2   tablespoons olive oil
3   cloves garlic
1   medium onion, about 8 ounces
4   ounces shiitake mushrooms, preferably without stems
1   10-ounce package frozen leaf or chopped spinach
1   pound lean ground sirloin
1   tablespoon fresh thyme leaves or 1 teaspoon dried thyme
    Salt and freshly ground black pepper
4   large eggs
¼   cup grated Parmesan cheese

1 Put the oil in a large, heavy skillet over medium-high heat. Peel the garlic. Peel and quarter the onion. Put the garlic and onion in a food processor and pulse just until chopped. Add to the skillet, stir, and cook while you remove and discard the stems, if any, from the mushrooms. Thinly slice the mushroom caps and add them to the skillet. Raise the heat to high, stir, and cook for about 3 minutes, until the onions turn translucent and the mushrooms soften. Scrape into a large mixing bowl.

2 Meanwhile, run the hot-water tap and remove the spinach from the package. Put the spinach and 2 tablespoons hot tap water in a microwave-safe container, cover, and cook in a microwave oven on high power for 5 minutes until defrosted. (Or put the spinach and ½ cup hot water in a 2-quart saucepan, cover, and cook on the stovetop over medium-high heat for 5 minutes.)

3 Add the beef to the same skillet used for the onion-mushroom mixture. Cook over high heat, breaking up any clumps, for about 3 minutes, just until the beef loses any redness.

4 While the beef cooks, drain the spinach and coarsely chop. Add the spinach to the mushroom mixture. If using fresh thyme, chop the leaves from the sprigs. (If using dried thyme, crush between your fingers.) Add the thyme to the mushroom-spinach mixture along with salt and pepper to taste. Mix well. Beat the eggs in a small bowl with the Parmesan cheese, salt, and pepper.

5 Add the mushroom-spinach mixture to the beef in the skillet. Mix well and reduce the heat to medium. Add the eggs and stir to spread the mixture evenly in the skillet. Cook for 3 to 4 minutes, just until the eggs are set. Serve directly from the skillet.

This San Francisco favorite was allegedly created at Little Joe's restaurant. Although it looks like a mish-mash your preteen children might create, it's delicious, especially when jazzed up with shiitake mushrooms, though plain white mushrooms would be fine. Serve with sourdough bread for additional San Francisco authenticity.

Serves 4

107

huevos rancheros with spicy black beans

3	**tablespoons peanut or canola oil**
1/2	**cup drained, diced canned tomatoes**
1/2	**cup commercial medium or hot tomato salsa**
1	**19-ounce can black beans**
3	**flour tortillas, 8 to 9 inches in diameter**
2	**tablespoons sliced pickled jalapeño peppers plus 1 tablespoon pickling juice, or 1 fresh jalapeño pepper and 1 tablespoon cider vinegar**
1/2	**small sweet onion such as a Vidalia**
6	**large eggs**
6	**sprigs cilantro**
1	**teaspoon chili powder**
	Salt

What I like about my version of this dish is that it doesn't look like a combination plate from a Tex-Mex joint. I got the idea for a quick ranchero sauce from The Feast of Santa Fe *by Huntley Dent, a fine southwestern cookbook. Adjust the heat to your taste with hotter or milder salsa and by adjusting the amount of jalapeños.*

Serves 3

1 Put the oil in a large, heavy skillet over medium-high heat. For the ranchero sauce, combine the tomatoes and salsa in a small saucepan over medium-low heat.

2 Reduce the heat under the skillet to medium and fry each tortilla for 1 minute on each side, until lightly browned. Put the tortillas on a plate and cover to keep warm. Meanwhile, open the can of beans into a colander, rinse, and drain briefly. Chop the pickled jalapeño and put into a mixing bowl with the pickling juice and the drained beans. (If using a fresh jalapeño, seed, stem, mince, and add to the beans with the cider vinegar.) Peel and chop the onion. You should have about ⅓ cup. Add to the beans.

3 Break the eggs into the same skillet used for the tortillas, cover, and fry over medium heat for 3 to 4 minutes, or until the yolks are set. Meanwhile, chop the leaves from the cilantro sprigs. Add the cilantro, chili powder, and salt to taste to the beans. Mix well.

4 Put one tortilla on each of 3 plates. Slide 2 eggs on each tortilla. Put two small mounds of beans on opposite sides of the tortilla, next to the eggs. Top the eggs with the ranchero sauce.

SOUPS

SOUPS in fifteen minutes? Yep, but these are not the kind that gurgle all day on the back of the stove. They are quicker and lighter but still full of flavor. And they're made from scratch, though I do judiciously use convenience ingredients, such as canned chicken stock and bottled clam juice.

Oyster and Spinach Stew (page 114), which is really more of a soup despite its name, uses fresh oysters and fresh spinach. Corn Chowder with Crabmeat and Pimientos (page 113) uses fresh corn and fresh crabmeat. And Endless Gazpacho in the Vegetarian chapter (page 120) has fresh tomatoes, cucumbers, corn, and zucchini.

When making fifteen-minute soups, you absolutely need a deep skillet, one with at least a four-quart capacity. This gives you a wide cooking surface that heats the soup much faster than soup pots or saucepans. The skillet should also have a cover—to increase the pressure inside the pan and thus make cooking go faster—and a heavy bottom to prevent burning.

Generally, the stock for these soups needs to get hot fairly quickly. However, milk can scorch over high heat, so I warm it separately over more moderate heat while I'm performing another task, like sautéing vegetables over high heat.

Because quick soups don't have the time to develop the deep flavors that longer-cooking soups have, you sometimes need to pump up the seasonings. For example, Clam Chowder with Potatoes and Bacon (page 115) has four bay leaves. Moroccan Chicken Soup (page 116) has a tablespoon each of ground cumin and ground ginger. This is not true for hot pepper like cayenne. Hot is hot from the get go.

When experimenting on your own, think of what food combinations go well together and toss them into stock, just as you might add them to pasta. If you like beans and greens, you might combine chopped kale and cannellini beans in a stock, perhaps with some chopped kielbasa. Garlicky chickpeas and tomatoes make a nice pasta sauce. So why not add them and broken up pasta strands to chicken stock for a quick, hearty soup?

bean soup with pasta and escarole

5½	cups chicken stock
8-12	ounces Italian-style veal or pork sausage
1	small head escarole, about 12 ounces
½	cup acini di pepe, pastina, or other tiny pasta for soups
	Salt
2	15-ounce cans cannellini beans
	Freshly ground black pepper
⅓	cup grated Parmesan cheese

1 Put the stock in a wide saucepan or deep skillet over high heat, cover, and bring to a boil, about 7 minutes. While the hot-water tap runs, put the sausages in a large, heavy skillet. Add ½ cup hot tap water, cover, and put over high heat. Cook for about 4 minutes, depending on the thickness of the sausages. Uncover and cook for about 4 minutes longer, until the water evaporates and the sausages are lightly browned and have no pink in the center. Turn the sausages once or twice to brown evenly.

2 While the stock comes to a boil and the sausages cook, fill the sink with cold water. Cut and discard the bottom ½ inch from the escarole. Cut the remainder crosswise into ½-inch-wide strips. Wash the escarole briefly in the sink and drain in a colander.

3 As soon as the stock comes to a boil, add the pasta and salt to taste (the amount will depend on how much salt is in the stock). Stir, cover, and return to a boil. Add the escarole to the soup.

4 Open the beans into the same colander used for the escarole, rinse, and drain briefly. Add to the soup. Cut the cooked sausage crosswise into ½-inch-wide rounds and add to the soup with salt and pepper to taste. Just before the 15 minutes are up, add the cheese and stir. Serve in soup plates garnished with additional pepper.

A member of the chicory family, escarole isn't commonly used outside of Italian cooking, but don't let the Italians have all the fun. Escarole's pleasant bitterness makes a nice contrast to the beans and pasta in this soup. If you don't eat veal or pork, poultry sausage with Italian seasonings can be used.

Serves 4

corn chowder with crabmeat and pimientos

1½	tablespoons unsalted butter
6	scallions
2	ribs celery
3	large or 4 small to medium ears fresh corn or 2 cups frozen corn kernels (about one 10-ounce package)
4	cups milk
1	4-ounce jar whole pimientos or roasted red bell peppers
½	pound jumbo lump crabmeat
8	sprigs parsley, preferably flat-leaf
¼	cup dry sherry
	Salt and freshly ground black pepper

1   Put the butter in a deep, heavy skillet over medium-high heat. Trim the scallions and celery and cut each crosswise into 4 pieces. Put in a food processor and pulse just until chopped. Add to the skillet, raise the heat to high, stir, and cook for 2 minutes, or until barely softened.

2   Meanwhile, husk the corn and cut off the kernels but do not discard the cobs. To remove the kernels, stand each ear on end and, beginning at the middle, cut down all around the cob. Then reverse the ends and repeat. (If using frozen corn, empty the box into a colander and let hot tap water run over the corn for 1 to 2 minutes, or until defrosted.)

3   Add the kernels to the skillet and stir. Add the milk. Chop the pimientos. Add to the skillet. Stir, cover, and bring just to a boil, then reduce the heat and let simmer, stirring several times.

4   Meanwhile, take the back of a chef's knife and rub it against the cobs over the skillet to remove the flavorful "milk." Add the crab and stir.

5   Chop the leaves from the parsley sprigs. Add the parsley, sherry, and salt and pepper to taste to the chowder and cook for 3 to 4 minutes. Taste, adjust the seasonings, and serve in soup plates.

A terrific dish for late summer when local corn is at its peak. It is almost as good made with frozen corn in the middle of January. Serve with crackers or crusty bread.

Serves 4

oyster and spinach stew

This satisfying stew is rich without being heavy. Crush some saltines into your bowl and go to town. If you can't get cleaned spinach in bags, use frozen leaf spinach. Loose spinach in bunches takes too much time to clean.

Serves 4

2	cups milk
2	cups half-and-half
1	teaspoon cayenne pepper
1	tablespoon Worcestershire sauce
	Salt and freshly ground black pepper
2	tablespoons unsalted butter
2	ten-ounce bags cleaned fresh spinach or 1½ ten-ounce boxes frozen leaf spinach
36	shucked oysters in their liquor
	Saltine crackers

1 Put the milk, half-and-half, cayenne, Worcestershire, and salt and pepper to taste in a heavy saucepan over medium heat to warm. Do not let boil. Put the butter in a deep, heavy skillet or Dutch oven over low heat.

2 Meanwhile, quickly pick through the spinach, discarding any damaged leaves or thick stems. Coarsely chop and put into a large colander. Rinse briefly, then add to the skillet without draining. (If using frozen spinach, put in a microwave-safe container with 3 tablespoons water, cover, and cook in a microwave oven on high power for 5 minutes until defrosted. Then coarsely chop.) Raise the heat to medium-high, cover, and cook for about 3 minutes, or until the spinach has barely wilted.

3 Add the oysters and their liquor and the warmed milk mixture to the skillet. Cover and bring to a bare simmer over medium-high heat, stirring a few times. Do not let boil. Cook for 5 minutes and adjust the seasoning as desired. Serve in soup plates with the saltine crackers.

clam chowder with potatoes and bacon

1	pound small red-skinned potatoes (no more than 1½ inches in diameter)
1	teaspoon salt, plus more to taste
4	ounces bacon, about 6 strips
1	medium onion, about 8 ounces
2	ribs celery
3	8-ounce bottles clam juice
3	6½-ounce cans chopped clams
1	tablespoon fresh thyme leaves or 1 teaspoon dried thyme
4	bay leaves
	Cayenne pepper
1½	cups half-and-half
	Freshly ground black pepper

1 While the hot-water tap runs, halve each potato (do not peel), then cut each half into 4 to 6 pieces, or into 2 to 4 pieces if the potatoes are very small. Put the potatoes and 1 teaspoon salt in large saucepan or deep skillet and barely cover the potatoes with hot tap water. Cover and cook over high heat for 10 minutes, or just until tender. Drain.

2 While the potatoes cook, put a deep, heavy skillet over high heat. Cut the bacon into 1-inch pieces. Add to the skillet and stir, breaking up any clumps. Peel and quarter the onion. Trim the celery ribs and cut each crosswise into 4 pieces. Put the onion and celery in a food processor and pulse just until chopped. Add to the skillet and cook for 3 minutes.

3 While the onion and celery cook, open the bottles of clam juice and cans of clams. Chop the thyme leaves. (If using dried thyme, crush between your fingers.) Add the clam juice, clams, thyme, bay leaves, and cayenne to taste to the skillet. Cover and bring to a boil. Meanwhile, put the half-and-half in a small saucepan and warm over medium heat.

4 As soon as the clam mixture boils, add the half-and-half and salt and pepper to taste. Bring just to, but not quite, a boil, stirring once or twice. Add the potatoes and bring the soup to a simmer. Simmer for 1 minute. Taste and adjust the seasonings. Discard the bay leaves and serve in soup plates.

This hearty soup is a great choice for a chilly evening, accompanied by oyster crackers and a lager beer. It has an authentic clam chowder texture, meaning it's lightly creamy, not thick and pasty like so many versions of clam chowder.

Serves 4

115

moroccan chicken soup

I love the exotic smells and flavors of Moroccan cuisine. This dish was inspired by my collaboration with chef Matthew Kenney—a real Moroccan food devotee—on our book Matthew Kenney's Mediterranean Cooking. *Serve it with pocketless pita bread or other flatbread.*

Serves 4

2	tablespoons olive oil
3	boneless, skinless chicken breast halves, about 6 ounces each, or 18 ounces chicken tenders
1	medium onion, about 8 ounces
1	tablespoon ground cumin
1	tablespoon ground ginger
1	teaspoon hot paprika or ¾ teaspoon sweet paprika and ¼ teaspoon cayenne pepper
5	cups chicken stock
2	medium zucchini, about 12 ounces
½	cup instant couscous
1	16-ounce can chickpeas
	Salt and freshly ground black pepper
8	sprigs cilantro

1 Put the oil in a deep, heavy skillet over medium-high heat. Cut the chicken into ½- to ¾-inch cubes. Add to the skillet, raise the heat to high, and stir once or twice.

2 While the chicken browns, peel and quarter the onion and put in a food processor. Pulse until just chopped. Add the onion, cumin, ginger, and paprika to the skillet. Stir and cook for 1 minute. Add the stock to the skillet and stir with a wide wooden spoon, scraping any bits from the bottom. Cover and bring to a boil, about 2 minutes.

3 Meanwhile, trim the zucchini and slice in half lengthwise. Then cut crosswise into ¼-inch-wide half-moons. When the soup comes to a boil, add the zucchini and the couscous to the skillet, stir, and cover.

4 Open the can of chickpeas into a small colander, rinse, and drain briefly. Add to the skillet. Cover and let the soup return to a boil, then lower the heat slightly so the soup simmers briskly for 4 minutes. Season with salt and pepper to taste. Chop the leaves from the cilantro sprigs. Stir into the soup, cook for 1 minute, and serve in soup plates.

VEGETARIAN

WHEN I lived in Oakland, California, I shopped regularly at the Berkeley Bowl, the best produce market I've ever seen. I remember thinking that I could easily become a vegetarian with the Berkeley Bowl nearby.

Alas, many of us don't have access to produce markets like the Berkeley Bowl. Still, getting more vegetables into our diet is important because nutritionists tell us to cut back on our consumption of red meats and other sources of saturated fat, and many vegetables have disease-fighting properties. Eating a meatless meal once or twice a week—especially one that doesn't require a lot of time to prepare—is a good way to do that. The six vegetarian dishes in this chapter should in no way be considered sacrifices or accommodations to your cardiologist. I doubt that you'll feel less satisfied after one of these meals than after the meals with meat elsewhere in the book.

With the exception of the small amounts of butter and cheese in Provençal Mushroom Ragout with Polenta (page 122) and the optional goat cheese in Four-Bean Salad with Arugula and Red Onion (page 127), there are no dairy products. So vegans can feel right at home. Even the ragout can be prepared without the cheese and butter, though I'd probably add a tablespoon of oil to the polenta to give it a smooth texture and rich flavor.

If these recipes inspire you to try a few fifteen-minute vegetarian dishes on your own, keep in mind four things. First, you'll need protein substitutes. Canned or frozen beans are the logical first choice, and they are used extensively here and elsewhere in the book. I keep at least three varieties of canned beans—chickpeas, black beans, and cannellini beans—and at least one frozen bean, usually limas, on hand at all times.

Second, go for "meaty" vegetables to sate the palate. Mushrooms, especially portobellos, are an excellent choice. So is broccoli, which is surprisingly high in protein. A 5.3-ounce serving (about one medium stalk) contains 5 grams of protein. Liberal seasoning will also help to satisfy the taste buds.

Third, seek out the freshest produce available, even if it means selecting something you hadn't intended to buy, much as you would shop for seafood. Why purchase shriveled string beans if the broccoli looks much better? Better to change the recipe than to use a vegetable that isn't appetizing or nutritionally sound. Buying what is in season is always preferable, and patronizing local farmers' markets even better, though most of the vegetables used in this chapter are available year-round in supermarkets.

Finally, there should be an underpinning of carbohydrates. It could be polenta, as in Provençal Mushroom Ragout with Polenta; rice, as in Salad Bar Stir-Fry with Basmati Rice (page 130); or bread and potatoes, as in Portobello Burgers with Fried Potatoes (page 128). Of course, pasta probably serves as a carbohydrate complement better than any of the above. Penne with Broccoli, Garlic, and Pecorino (page 92) in the Pasta and Grains chapter could easily be made vegetarian by eliminating the anchovies.

Other recipes in the book could be converted to vegetarian dishes. In the Chili with Beans in the Meat chapter (page 39), mushrooms could be substituted for the beef and another type of bean could be added. Tuscan Tomato and Bread Salad (page 134) in the Salad chapter contains tuna, but it was a vegetarian dish in its original form. And a good case could be made for a vegetarian version of Pantry Antipasto (page 136) by eliminating the tuna and increasing the cheese and eggs.

endless gazpacho

I call this cool and soothing soup "endless" gazpacho because there's almost no limit to what you can include from summer's bounty. To cool the soup faster put the V-8 juice in the refrigerator before you go to work. The same logic applies to ingredients for any cold soup.

Serves 4

3	**ears fresh corn**
1	**medium to large mild red onion or sweet onion such as Vidalia, 8 to 12 ounces**
2	**Kirby or small pickling cucumbers**
2	**pounds very ripe tomatoes**
2	**small yellow squash or zucchini**
2	**small ribs celery**
1	**19-ounce can black beans**
8-10	**sprigs cilantro**
4	**cups V-8 or tomato juice**
	Salt and freshly ground black pepper
	Hot-pepper sauce

1 While the hot-water tap runs, husk the corn. Put the corn and 4 cups hot tap water in a large pot. Cover and cook over high heat for 5 minutes. Drain and run under cold water to cool.

2 Meanwhile, peel and quarter the onion. Trim the ends of the cucumbers and quarter (no need to peel). Put the onion and cucumbers in a food processor and purée until not quite smooth. Core and quarter the tomatoes. Add to the processor and purée. (The puréeing could also be done in a blender.) Remove the gazpacho to a large mixing bowl (preferably metal) and put the bowl in the freezer (or put in a larger bowl half filled with ice and water) while you trim and dice the squash and celery.

3 To remove the kernels, stand each ear of corn on end and, beginning at the middle, cut down all around the cob. Then reverse the ends and repeat. Add the corn to the soup.

4 Open the can of beans into a colander, rinse, and drain briefly. Chop the leaves from the cilantro sprigs. Add beans, cilantro leaves, and V-8 juice to the soup and mix well. Season with salt, black pepper, and hot-pepper sauce to taste.

provençal mushroom ragout with polenta

Ragouts traditionally mean hefty, long-simmering meat stews. In recent years, chefs have slapped the ragout label on quick vegetable stews like this one. I use large white mush-rooms or light beige portobellos.Otherwise, the ragout will be unattractively dark. Because markets leave portobellos exposed to air all day, they can get quite dark, so buy them earlier in the day.

Serves 4

2	tablespoons olive oil
1	medium to large onion, 8 to 12 ounces
1	red bell pepper
1	pound large white mushrooms or light-colored portobello mushrooms
1	medium to large tomato, about 12 ounces
1	teaspoon salt, plus more to taste
12	large basil leaves
	Freshly ground black pepper
1½	cups instant polenta
2	tablespoons unsalted butter
¼	cup grated Parmesan cheese

1   Put the oil in a large, deep, heavy skillet or wok over medium heat. Cut off a thin slice from the top and bottom of the onion, halve lengthwise, peel each half, and cut cross-wise into thin half-moon slices. Cut the top from the bell pepper. Stand it upright and cut down inside the four walls, separating them from the center core and seeds. Then cut the walls into thin strips. Add the onion and pepper to the skillet, raise the heat to high, and stir.

2   Halve the white mushrooms if they are particularly large, then cut into ¼-inch-thick slices. (If using portobello mushrooms, remove the stems from the caps, and cut the caps in half. Cut the caps crosswise into ¼-inch-thick slices. Cut the bottom ½ inch from the stems and coarsely chop the rest.) Add to the skillet and stir. Cut the tomato in half lengthwise, gently squeeze out some of the juice and seeds, and cut each half into wedges, removing the core. Add to the skillet, stir well, cover, and cook for 4 minutes. Then uncover, reduce the heat to medium, and cook for another 4 minutes.

3   Meanwhile, run the hot-water tap and put 3¾ cups hot tap water and 1 teaspoon salt in a heavy saucepan. Cover and bring to a boil over high heat, about 2 minutes. While the polenta water comes to a boil, stack the basil leaves, then roll and cut crosswise into thin ribbons. You should have about ¼ cup. Add the basil and salt and pepper to taste to the mushroom mixture.

4   When the polenta water comes to a boil, gradually pour in the polenta. Reduce the heat to medium and stir periodically with a firm whisk or wooden spoon for about 3 minutes, or until the polenta thickens and loses its grainy taste. Stir in the butter and cheese. Pour the polenta onto a serving platter or onto individual soup plates. Spoon the mushroom ragout over the polenta.

curried vegetable stew with bruschetta

4	tablespoons extra-virgin olive oil
1	large sweet potato, about 12 ounces
1	large onion, about 12 ounces
3	medium zucchini
1	tablespoon curry powder
1	medium red bell pepper
2	cups vegetable stock or water
1	10-ounce package frozen baby lima beans
8	ounces small green beans, preferably haricots verts
$\frac{1}{4}$	teaspoon saffron threads
	Salt and freshly ground black pepper
1	small round loaf sourdough bread
2	tablespoons sesame seeds

While I like all the recipes in this chapter, this one is my favorite. In fact, it's one of my favorites in the entire book because of the interplay of the spices with the colors, flavors, and textures of the vegetables.

Serves 4

1 Turn on the broiler and adjust the broiler pan so it is 6 inches from the heat source. Put 2 tablespoons of the oil a large, deep, heavy skillet or Dutch oven over medium-high heat. Peel the sweet potato and halve lengthwise, then cut each piece in half crosswise. Put the 4 pieces into a food processor with the slicing attachment and slice. (Or chop by hand.) Add to the skillet and stir.

2 Cut off a thin slice from the top and bottom of the onion, halve lengthwise, and peel each half. Trim the ends from the zucchini. Slice the onion and zucchini using the slicing attachment of the food processor. (Or chop by hand.) Add the onion, zucchini, and curry powder to the skillet. Stir well. Cut the top from the bell pepper. Stand it upright and cut down inside the four walls, separating them from the center core and seeds. Then cut the walls into thin strips. Add the bell pepper and stock to the skillet, stir, cover, and bring to a boil over high heat.

CONTINUED

curried vegetable stew with bruschetta

3   Meanwhile, put the lima beans in a colander and run hot tap water over them until defrosted. Trim the stem ends from the green beans. Add both beans to the skillet. Crush the saffron threads with your fingers over the stew and season with salt and pepper to taste. Cook, covered, for 7 minutes, stirring periodically, until the beans are just tender.

4   While the stew cooks, trim the ends from the bread, cut four ½-inch-thick slices from what remains, and put them on a baking sheet. Put in the broiler for about 3 minutes, turning once, until lightly toasted. While the bread toasts, put the sesame seeds in a heavy skillet over medium-high heat and stir frequently until lightly toasted, about 3 minutes. Ladle the stew into soup plates and sprinkle with the sesame seeds. Brush the toasted bread with the remaining 2 tablespoons oil and serve one slice on each plate.

four-bean salad with arugula and red onion

	Salt
12	**ounces small green beans, preferably haricots verts**
1	**bunch arugula**
1	**15-ounce can red kidney beans**
1	**15-ounce can black beans**
1	**15-ounce can chickpeas**
1	**mild medium red onion or sweet onion such as Vidalia, about 8 ounces**
1	**large tomato, about 12 ounces**
1	**clove garlic**
12	**basil leaves**
2½	**tablespoons red wine vinegar**
	Freshly ground black pepper
⅓	**cup extra-virgin olive oil**
6	**ounces goat cheese or feta cheese (optional)**

While this colorful and delicious salad is sufficiently filling as is, you can add cubes of goat or feta cheese to bulk up the protein if you feel the need. Chewy country bread is a good accompaniment.

Serves 4

1   Run the hot-water tap and put a healthy pinch of salt and 2 cups hot tap water in a skillet. Cover and put over high heat until the water comes to a boil. Meanwhile, fill the sink with cold water and trim the stem ends from the green beans. When the water boils, add the green beans to the skillet, cover, and cook for 3 minutes if the beans are small, 5 minutes if larger, or until just tender. Drain into a colander and rinse briefly with cold water to cool.

2   Meanwhile, cut the arugula crosswise into ½-inch-wide strips, discarding the stems. Wash the arugula briefly but vigorously in the sink to remove grit. Then spin the greens dry in a salad spinner. Remove any excess moisture with paper towels.

3   Open all the cans of beans into a colander, rinse, and drain briefly. While they drain, cut off a thin slice from the top and bottom of the onion, halve lengthwise, peel each half, and cut crosswise into thin half-moon slices. Cut the tomato in half lengthwise, gently squeeze out some of the juice and seeds, and cut each half into thin wedges, removing the core. Put the canned beans, onion, tomato, and green beans in a large mixing bowl.

4   Peel the garlic and drop down the chute of a food processor with the motor running. When it is puréed, stop the motor and scrape down the sides of the bowl with a rubber spatula. Add the basil, vinegar, and salt and pepper to taste. Turn on the processor again and gradually pour in the oil through the chute. Add the dressing to the vegetables and mix well. If desired, crumble the cheese and fold into the salad.

portobello burgers with fried potatoes

I'd rather eat this
burger than one
made of beef. It's
tastier and less filling
than a traditional
hamburger, and
healthier too!

Serves 4

8	tablespoons extra-virgin olive oil
2	large red-skinned potatoes, about 1 pound
2	cloves garlic
½	teaspoon dried thyme
2	tablespoons balsamic vinegar
	Salt and freshly ground black pepper
4	portobello mushroom caps, about 5 ounces each
1	medium green bell pepper
2	small to medium sweet onions such as Vidalia, 4 to 8 ounces each
1	teaspoon paprika
4	sesame seed hamburger buns
¼	cup commercial mayonnaise
1	tablespoon drained small capers
1	medium tomato, about 8 ounces
4	large lettuce leaves

1   Turn on the broiler and adjust the broiler pan so it is as close to the heat source as possible. Put 2 tablespoons of the oil in a large, heavy skillet over medium-high heat. Halve the potatoes lengthwise, thinly slice crosswise, and add to the skillet. Cook for 5 minutes, stirring a few times.

2   While the potatoes cook, peel the garlic. Drop down the chute of a food processor with the motor running. Stop the motor and scrape down the sides of the bowl with a rubber spatula. Add the thyme, vinegar, the remaining 6 tablespoons of oil, and salt and pepper to taste. Turn on the processor and mix until the dressing is combined. Put the mushroom caps in a shallow baking pan just large enough to hold them in one layer. Brush one side of the caps with half of the olive oil mixture, put in the broiler, and cook for 5 minutes. Turn the caps, brush the other side with the remaining olive oil mixture, and cook for 4 more minutes. When done, the caps should be lightly charred and just beginning to soften.

3   Meanwhile, cut the top from the bell pepper. Stand it upright and cut down inside the four walls, separating them from the center core and seeds. Then cut the walls into thin strips. Add to the potatoes and stir. Cut off a thin slice from the top and bottom of one of the onions, halve lengthwise, peel each half, and cut crosswise into thin half-moon slices. Add the onion, paprika, and salt and pepper to taste to the potatoes and mix well. Reduce the heat to medium and stir periodically to prevent burning. Cook until the mushroom caps are done.

4   While the potatoes and mushrooms are cooking, open the buns and put them on a baking sheet. Put them in the oven to toast lightly. Mix the mayonnaise and capers in a small bowl. Core and slice the tomato. Peel the remaining onion and thinly slice into rings.

5   Spread each of the buns with 1 tablespoon caper mayonnaise. Place a lettuce leaf, a slice of tomato, and a slice of onion on the top half of each bun. Put a mushroom cap on the bottom half. Serve with the potatoes.

salad bar stir-fry with basmati rice

A stir-fried salad? Not exactly. This is a vegetable stir-fry that utilizes the convenience of a supermarket salad bar, which has a large selection of already cut up raw vegetables—many of which don't belong in salads, frankly. So very little chopping is needed. Choose ten of the suggestions listed, substituting freely, depending on how good your local salad bar is. Amounts are approximate, and you can double up on your favorite items.

Serves 4

1	cup basmati rice
	Salt
1	2½-inch piece fresh ginger
4	teaspoons soy sauce
3	tablespoons dry sherry or rice wine
1	tablespoon toasted sesame oil
1	cup vegetable stock or water
½	teaspoon hot-pepper flakes, or to taste
2	teaspoons cornstarch
2	tablespoons peanut oil
1	cup sliced onions
1	cup bell pepper rings
1	cup broccoli florets, the smaller the better
1	cup cauliflower florets, the smaller the better
1	cup chopped celery
1	cup shredded red cabbage
1	cup sliced or shredded carrots
1	cup sliced water chestnuts
1	cup sliced mushrooms
1	cup bean sprouts
1	cup spinach leaves (optional)
1	cup whole baby corn (optional)
¼	cup pumpkin seeds or other seeds or nuts

1   While the hot-water tap runs, put the rice in a 2-quart saucepan. Add 2 cups hot tap water and 1 teaspoon salt. Bring to a boil over high heat, then reduce the heat to low, cover and cook for 10 minutes. Turn off the heat and keep covered until ready to serve. (Or put the rice, 2 cups hot water, and 1 teaspoon salt in a 2-quart microwave-safe container. Cover and cook in a microwave oven on high power for 10 minutes. Keep covered until ready to serve.)

2   Meanwhile, peel and halve the ginger. Drop the ginger down the chute of a food processor with the motor running and purée while you mix the soy sauce, sherry, sesame oil, and stock in a cup.

3   Stop the motor and scrape down the sides of the bowl. Add the hot-pepper flakes and cornstarch. Add the soy sauce mixture through the chute of the processor with the motor running and process until the mixture is combined.

4   Put the peanut oil in a wok or a large, heavy skillet over medium-high heat. If the onions and bell peppers are in rings, cut the rings in the half. Add the onions, bell pepper, broccoli, cauliflower, celery, red cabbage, and sliced carrots to the wok. (Wait a minute or two to add the carrots if they are shredded.) Stir for 2 minutes.

5   Add the water chestnuts and mushrooms and stir for 2 minutes. Add the sprouts and, if using, the spinach and baby corn. Cook for 3 minutes. Season to taste with salt. Add the cornstarch mixture and stir well. Cook, stirring, for about 1 minute, or until the sauce thickens. Check for salt and pour onto a platter. Sprinkle with seeds or nuts. Serve with the rice. (Keep the stir-fry covered if it is done before the 15 minutes are up and the rice has had a chance to fully steam.)

SALADS & COLD PLATTERS

REMEMBER when salad was merely one component of the meal: just a few greens, some tomato wedges, and sliced cucumbers tossed with bottled dressing? Sometimes, it was even more basic, like those hearts of lettuce drowned in Russian dressing that were served all too often at hotel banquets.

Now salads can *be* the meal and contain almost anything, from shrimp to water chestnuts. This makes our choices for quick meals much greater. As is true with the other recipes in this book, the salads in this chapter have been designed to be eaten as main courses. In some cases I have taken salads not normally thought of as main courses and built them up so they can be meals in themselves. For instance, Tuscan Tomato and Bread Salad (page 134) with the addition of tuna becomes a summer lunch or dinner.

I invite you to experiment by turning lighter salads you normally eat into one-dish meals. This usually means adding protein such as meat, poultry, seafood, cheese, eggs, or legumes. Main-Course Caesar Salad (page 139), for example, gets a topping of rock shrimp. Perhaps a dozen years ago, restaurants started putting all manner of meat, poultry, and seafood on Caesar salad to turn it into a main dish. I've even had sweetbreads atop those romaine leaves.

In addition to introducing protein, you can also increase the amount of protein that's already there to make a salad more substantial. In Curly Endive with Pancetta and Blue Cheese (page 141), I added more blue cheese and pancetta to the amount in the French original (which used bacon instead of pancetta).

Salads don't have to be cold. Warm salads have become more popular in restaurants in recent years, and they give cooks more flexibility with ingredients. So why shouldn't we take advantage of this at home? Warm Shrimp and White Bean Salad with Red Potatoes (page 144), Asian Sesame Chicken Salad (page 145), and Red Cabbage, Bean, and Sausage Salad with Toasted Fennel (page 149) are all examples of this.

Salads made with grains can also make a meal in a hurry when you use quick-cooking grains like the instant couscous used in Couscous with Mergez Sausage (page 100) in the Pasta and Grains chapter. Though not a true salad, it could be if the sausage were cut up and mixed into the couscous instead of being served on the side. Such a salad would also work with chickpeas or other legumes, chicken, or seafood instead of the sausage. Other quick-cooking grains could be used as well, like the brown rice used in the Seafood Pilaf with Saffron and Peas (page 98), also in the Pasta and Grains chapter.

There is a bit of a misconception that cold salads are always faster than traditional hot dishes because they don't have to be cooked. However, for cold salads, many of the ingredients have to be cut or chopped, which takes time. Salad greens have to be washed, and sometimes quite thoroughly in the case of arugula and endive. But as I said in the Flavor, Organization, Focus, and Creativity chapter, convenience foods can make this process move along more quickly. Already cleaned and shredded cabbage, available from the supermarket salad bar or bagged in the produce section, could be used for the Red Cabbage, Bean Salad, and Sausage Salad with Toasted Fennel. Canned beans help make Warm Shrimp and White Bean Salad with Red Potatoes a snap.

Convenience appliances, particularly the food processor, also speed up salad making. Though I've owned a food processor for many years, until I wrote this book I used it mainly for purées and such. Now I consider it indispensable for shredding cabbage in Red Cabbage, Bean Salad, and Sausage Salad with Toasted Fennel and making dressings in Main-Course Caesar Salad and Salade Niçoise (page 142). The mandoline, an angled metal cutter with adjustable blades, shreds, slices, and juliennes almost as easily as—and with more accuracy than—a food processor, though it doesn't dice. Sharp knives are invaluable too. A salad spinner is important because it works quickly and efficiently at removing moisture from salad greens. Greens and other vegetables must be dry so dressing adequately clings to them.

Another important piece of equipment you need for making fifteen-minute main-course salads is a sufficiently large mixing bowl. One that is too small makes it impossible to quickly combine all the ingredients without some spilling out. If necessary, a large cooking pot will do.

For cold salads, don't be afraid to mix with your hands. They are much more efficient than salad utensils.

Salads should take advantage of seasonal produce at its peak. Thus, it would be ridiculous to make Tuscan Tomato and Bread Salad unless you had ripe local tomatoes, or Salade Niçoise if the green beans were not top quality.

Because dressings are so important in salads, the quality of their ingredients is critical. Use only the best—meaning intensely flavored—oils and vinegars you can afford. Better to have one really good red wine or balsamic vinegar and one top-notch extra-virgin olive oil than four mediocre ones of each. Just as important are the seasonings, from freshly ground black pepper to fresh herbs.

tuscan tomato and bread salad

Italians never waste bread, which is why they created panzanella, the wonderful salad for leftover bread. Unlike a traditional panzanella, this salad doesn't have time to marinate and soften the dried bread. So you must use fresh bread, albeit one with some texture. I've added tuna packed in olive oil, which gives the dish added protein for a main course as well as a flavor boost.

Serves 4

1	loaf coarsely textured Italian country bread, about 1 pound
1½–2	pounds ripe tomatoes
1	tablespoon red wine vinegar
3	tablespoons extra–virgin olive oil
	Salt and freshly ground black pepper
1	medium cucumber
1	small to medium sweet onion such as Vidalia, 4 to 8 ounces
20	basil leaves
20	pitted Greek black olives such as kalamata or Italian black olives such as gaeta
2	tablespoons drained small capers
1	6–ounce can tuna packed in olive oil

1 Cut the bread into ¾-inch cubes and put in a large mixing bowl. Cut the tomato in half lengthwise. Gently squeeze out some of the juice and seeds into a small bowl; you should have at least ¼ cup. Cut each half into thin wedges, removing the core. Add the tomatoes to the bread.

2 Add the vinegar, olive oil, and salt and pepper to taste to the tomato juice (add a bit more oil and vinegar if you don't have enough juice) and stir well. Add the dressing to the bread and toss well.

3 Trim the ends from the cucumber, peel, halve lengthwise, and remove the seeds. (The easiest way to remove the seeds is to scoop them out with a teaspoon toward the end of the cucumber that appears more open than the other.) Cut each half crosswise into thin slices. Add to the bread mixture.

4 Cut off a thin slice from the top and bottom of the onion, halve lengthwise, peel each half, and cut crosswise into thin half-moon slices. Add to the bread mixture. Stack the basil leaves, roll, and cut crosswise into thin ribbons. You should have ¼ to ⅓ cup. Add all but 1 teaspoon of the basil to the bread mixture.

5 Coarsely chop the olives. Add the olives and 1 tablespoon of the capers to the bread mixture. Open the can of tuna, flake gently with a fork, and add to the bread mixture. Toss the salad well but gently with your hands. Sprinkle the top of the salad with the remaining basil and capers.

pantry antipasto

While this meal—
with the addition of
some crusty bread—
will serve four people
for dinner, you can
also serve it as hors
d'oeuvres for up to six
people. One caveat:
For this dish to be
done within fifteen
minutes, the eggs will
be slightly underdone
in the yolks and still
warm. That's fine
with me—and com-
pletely safe, by the
way. If you'd prefer
otherwise, cook them
a few minutes longer
or substitute with a
thinly sliced cured
meat such as salami
or prosciutto.

Serves 4

4	large eggs
1	15-ounce can cannellini beans
1/2	teaspoon dried sage leaves
5	tablespoons extra-virgin olive oil
	Salt and freshly ground black pepper
1	15-ounce can sliced beets
2	tablespoons sherry vinegar, raspberry vinegar, or other mild, fruity vinegar
4	chives
1	15-ounce can artichoke hearts packed in water
2	teaspoons dried mint
1/2	lemon
24	oil-cured or other black olives (not ripe olives)
	Hot-pepper flakes
1	small fennel bulb or 2 Kirby pickling cucumbers, about 12 ounces
1	7-ounce jar roasted red bell peppers
6-8	ounces Asiago or aged provolone cheese
2	6-ounce cans tuna packed in olive oil

1 While the hot-water tap runs, put the eggs in a small saucepan. Barely cover the eggs with hot tap water, cover the saucepan, and bring to a boil over high heat. When the water boils, reduce the heat to medium and cook for 8 minutes.

2 Meanwhile, open the can of cannellini beans into a colander, rinse, and drain briefly. Put the beans in a large mixing bowl with the sage leaves (crushed between your fingers), 2 tablespoons of the olive oil, and salt and pepper to taste. Mix well and scrape into a small serving bowl with a rubber spatula. Open the can of beets into the same colander and drain briefly. Put in the same mixing bowl with the vinegar, 1 tablespoon of the remaining olive oil, and salt and pepper to taste. Mix well and scrape into a small serving bowl with a rubber spatula. Chop the chives and sprinkle over the beets.

3   Open the can of artichoke hearts into the same colander and drain briefly. Halve length-wise and put in the same mixing bowl. Add the mint (crushed between your fingers), 2 tablespoons of the remaining olive oil, and salt and pepper to taste. Juice the lemon half and add to the artichokes. Mix well and scrape into a small serving bowl with a rubber spatula. In the same mixing bowl, toss the olives and a healthy pinch of hot pepper flakes. Put the olives in a small serving bowl.

4   Trim the green stalks from the top of the fennel bulb and cut $\frac{1}{4}$ inch from the bottom. Cut the remaining white bulb lengthwise into 4 slices, then cut into strips about $\frac{1}{2}$ inch wide. (If using cucumbers, trim and cut each lengthwise into 8 wedges.) Cut the roasted peppers into $\frac{1}{2}$-inch-wide strips. Cut the cheese into $\frac{1}{2}$-inch cubes.

5   Open the cans of tuna and arrange the tuna and cheese cubes at opposite ends of a large platter. Arrange the peppers next to the tuna and the fennel next to the cheese. Put the olives in the center of the platter. Drain the eggs, peel under cold running water, and halve lengthwise. Place, cut side up, throughout the platter. Surround the platter with the bowls of beans, beets, and artichokes.

main-course caesar salad

7	*tablespoons olive oil*
6	*slices French baguette, ½ inch thick, or 3 slices larger Italian bread, ½ inch thick*
1	*head romaine lettuce, about 1 ¼ pounds*
1	*clove garlic*
2	*anchovy fillets*
½	*lemon*
2	*teaspoons Dijon mustard*
1	*large egg yolk (see Note)*
1	*teaspoon Worcestershire sauce*
½	*teaspoon Tabasco sauce*
⅓	*cup grated Parmesan cheese*
	Salt and freshly ground black pepper
1	*pound shelled raw rock shrimp or other small shelled raw shrimp*

1 Put 2 tablespoons of the oil in a large, heavy skillet or wok over medium-high heat. Cut the bread into ½-inch cubes. Add the bread to the skillet, reduce the heat to medium-low, and cook for 4 to 5 minutes, tossing periodically, until just crisp. Reduce the heat if needed to prevent burning.

2 Meanwhile, cut ½ inch from the top and bottom of the romaine and cut the head cross-wise into 1-inch-wide strips. Put the strips in a salad spinner, fill with water, drain, and spin the greens dry. Remove any excess moisture with paper towels.

3 Peel the garlic. Drop the garlic and anchovies down the chute of a food processor with the motor running. Purée while you juice the lemon half. Stop the motor and scrape down the sides of the bowl with a rubber spatula. Add 2 tablespoons of the lemon juice and the mustard, egg yolk, Worcestershire, Tabasco, cheese, and salt and pepper to taste. With the motor running, gradually add 4 tablespoons of the remaining oil through the chute and process until the dressing is combined.

CONTINUED

Caesar Cardini, the inventor of the Caesar salad, is probably spinning in his grave at the thought of what we've done to his original. But adding meat and seafood has turned Caesar salads into meals instead of first courses, perfect for life in the fast lane. For this salad I use rock shrimp, tasty morsels with a crayfishlike flavor, usually sold already shelled. More traditional shrimp are an adequate substitute.

Serves 4

main–course caesar salad

4   Put the remaining 1 tablespoon of oil in a large, heavy skillet over high heat. Add the shrimp and season with salt and pepper. Cook for 2 to 3 minutes, tossing a few times to cook evenly, just until the shrimp firm up and their color changes.

5   While the shrimp cook, put the romaine in a large salad bowl. Add the dressing and toss well. Add the croutons and toss. Put the salad on individual plates and spread the cooked shrimp evenly on top.

Note: If you have concerns about using raw eggs, replace the egg in this recipe with ¼ cup egg substitute or 2 additional teaspoons of Dijon mustard.

curly endive with pancetta and blue cheese

1	**head curly endive, about 12 ounces**
8	**ounces sliced pancetta or bacon**
6	**slices French baguette, ½ inch thick, or 3 slices larger Italian bread, ½ inch thick**
⅓	**cup walnut or hazelnut oil**
2	**tablespoons sherry or red wine vinegar**
	Freshly ground black pepper
4	**ounces blue cheese**
½	**cup walnut pieces, about 2 ounces**

1 Fill the sink with cold water while you cut ½ inch from the bottom and the top of the endive. Remove any damaged leaves and cut the head crosswise into ½-inch-wide strips. Wash the endive briefly but vigorously to remove grit. Then spin dry in a salad spinner. Remove any excess moisture with paper towels.

2 Put a large skillet or wok over medium-high heat and cut the pancetta into strips ¼ to ½ inch wide. Add to the skillet, reduce the heat to medium, cover, and cook for 4 minutes, stirring periodically, until the fat is rendered and the pancetta is cooked. With a slotted spoon, remove the pancetta to a plate.

3 Meanwhile, cut the bread into ½ inch cubes. Add the bread to the skillet, reduce the heat to medium-low, and cook for 4 to 5 minutes, tossing periodically until just crisp. Reduce the heat if needed to prevent burning. While the bread cubes cook, mix the oil, vinegar, and pepper to taste in a cup.

4 Crumble or chop the blue cheese. You should have about 1 cup. Put the endive in a large mixing bowl. Add the dressing, blue cheese, and walnuts and toss well. Add the pancetta and croutons and toss again.

Hearty greens like curly endive (sometimes erroneously called chicory) are perfect for a quick main-course salad because they stand up to strong flavors like pancetta (Italian unsmoked bacon) and blue cheese. This salad doesn't need salt because the pancetta and blue cheese add enough. A crisp and fruity Riesling or gewürztraminer is a good wine match.

Serves 4

salad niçoise

It's important to note
that this French
classic is supposed to
be made with canned
tuna. That makes it a
good pantry salad.
Because the hard-
cooked eggs come with
the same caveat as
the Pantry Antipasto
(page 136), you may
want to consider
substituting one or
more of the following:
sliced cooked potatoes,
anchovies, capers,
julienned bell peppers,
or sweet onions.

Serves 4

4	**large eggs**
	Salt
1	**pound small green beans, preferably haricots verts**
1	**clove garlic**
12	**large basil leaves**
1	**tablespoon Dijon mustard**
	Freshly ground pepper
6	**tablespoons extra–virgin olive oil**
2	**tablespoons red wine vinegar**
5	**ounces mesclun or other salad mix, about 5 cups**
3	**6–ounce cans tuna packed in olive oil**
2	**medium ripe tomatoes, about 12 ounces**
30	**black olives, preferably oil–cured**

1   While the hot-water tap runs, put the eggs in a small saucepan. Barely cover the eggs with hot tap water, cover the saucepan, and bring to a boil over high heat. When the water boils, reduce the heat to medium and cook for 8 minutes.

2   Run the hot-water tap again and put a healthy pinch of salt and 4 cups hot tap water in a skillet. Cover and put over high heat while you trim the stem ends from the green beans. When the water boils, add the beans to the skillet, cover, and cook for 3 minutes if the beans are small, 5 minutes if larger, or until just tender. Drain into a colander and rinse briefly with cold water to cool.

3   While beans and eggs cook, peel the garlic. Drop down the chute of a food processor with the motor running and purée. Stop the motor and scrape down the sides of the bowl with a rubber spatula. Add the basil, mustard, and salt and pepper to taste. With the motor running, gradually add the oil and vinegar through the chute and process until the dressing is combined.

4   Put the salad mix in a salad spinner, fill with water, drain, and spin the greens dry. Remove any excess moisture with paper towels. Open the cans of tuna. Halve the tomatoes and cut each half into wedges.

5   Put the salad greens on a large platter. Place the tuna in the middle of the greens. Put the beans in 4 bundles radiating out from the tuna, like spokes. Put the tomato wedges in between the beans. Scatter the olives all around.

6   Drain the eggs, peel under cold running water, and halve lengthwise. Place, cut side up, throughout the platter. Drizzle the dressing over the entire salad, scraping it out of the processor bowl with rubber spatula.

warm shrimp and white bean salad with red potatoes

This amazingly simple salad has everything: beautiful color, nice contrasts in texture, and lots of flavor. You can substitute sea scallops for the shrimp if you like.

Serves 4

1	**pound large red-skinned potatoes**
1/3	**cup extra-virgin olive oil**
1	**pound shelled raw shrimp**
	Salt and freshly ground black pepper
1	**lemon**
1	**15-ounce can cannellini beans or other large white beans**
1	**4-ounce jar whole pimientos or roasted red bell peppers**
1	**small mild red onion or sweet onion such as Vidalia, about 4 ounces**
2	**ribs celery**
8	**fresh sage leaves or 1 teaspoon dried sage leaves**

1 While the hot-water tap runs, halve the potatoes lengthwise, then thinly slice crosswise (but do not peel). Put the potatoes in a large saucepan and barely cover with hot tap water. Cover and cook over high heat for 10 minutes, or until just tender.

2 Meanwhile, put the oil in a large, heavy skillet over high heat. Halve the shrimp crosswise if large, then season with salt and pepper. Add the shrimp to the skillet cook for 2 minutes, turning once halfway through, until the shrimp just begin to firm up and change color. Juice the lemon and add the juice to the skillet. Stir for 30 seconds, then turn off heat.

3 While the shrimp cook, open the can of beans into a colander, rinse, and drain briefly. Cut the pimientos into long, thin strips. Cut off a thin slice from the top and bottom of the onion, halve lengthwise, peel each half, and cut crosswise into thin half-moon slices. Trim the celery and cut crosswise on the diagonal into 1/4-inch-wide crescents.

4 Put the beans, peppers, onion, and celery in a large mixing bowl. Add the shrimp and, using a rubber spatula, scrape in the cooking liquid. Mince the fresh sage leaves. (If using dried sage, crush between your fingers.) Add the sage to the bowl and toss. Drain the potatoes and add to the bowl. Season with salt and pepper to taste and toss.

asian sesame chicken salad

1/3	**cup peanut oil**
2/3	**cup sesame seeds**
4	**boneless, skinless chicken breast halves, 5 to 6 ounces each, pounded evenly to about half their original thickness (by the butcher if possible)**
	Salt and freshly ground black pepper
1	**small head Chinese cabbage, 1 to 1 1/4 pounds**
1	**2-inch piece fresh ginger**
2	**tablespoons fish sauce or soy sauce**
2	**tablespoons rice wine vinegar**
2	**tablespoons toasted sesame oil**
1	**lime**
1	**8-ounce can sliced water chestnuts**
6	**scallions**
1	**medium red bell pepper**
10	**sprigs cilantro**

1   Put the peanut oil in a heavy skillet large enough to hold all the chicken in one layer without crowding. Put the skillet over medium-low heat. Spread the sesame seeds on a pie plate or wax paper. (If the butcher hasn't done so, pound the breasts between two sheets of aluminum foil or wax paper with the side of a cleaver or a meat pounder.) Season the breasts with salt and pepper and press into the sesame seeds to coat both sides evenly. Put in the skillet, raise the heat to medium-high, and cook for 5 minutes on each side, gently turning the breasts with a spatula, until the meat is firm and no pink shows in the middle. (Cut into one to check if you're not sure.) Reduce the heat if needed to prevent burning.

2   Meanwhile, trim the bottom ½ inch from the cabbage and remove any damaged or withered parts from the tops of the leaves. Cut crosswise into strips no more than ½ inch wide. Put into a salad spinner, fill with water, drain, and spin the greens dry. Remove any excess moisture with paper towels.

CONTINUED

If you like Chinese chicken salad, you'll love this variation of it. I prefer to make it with the taller, slimmer, more assertive variety of Chinese or celery cabbage, sometimes called Peking cabbage or Michihli cabbage. The milder and more common Napa cabbage is an adequate substitute. If neither is available, use an equivalent amount of romaine lettuce.

Serves 4

asian sesame chicken salad

3   Peel and halve the ginger. Drop down the chute of a food processor with the motor running and purée. Stop the motor and scrape down the sides of the bowl with a rubber spatula. Add the fish sauce, vinegar, and sesame oil. Juice the lime and add the juice to the ginger mixture. Process until the dressing is combined. Add salt to taste.

4   Open the can of water chestnuts and drain. Trim the scallions and cut the white and green parts crosswise into thin slices. Cut the top from the bell pepper. Stand it upright and cut down inside the four walls, separating them from the center core and seeds. Then cut the walls into thin strips. Coarsely chop the leaves from the cilantro sprigs.

5   Put the cabbage in a large mixing bowl. Add the water chestnuts, scallions, bell pepper, cilantro, and dressing. Toss well. Cut the cooked chicken into strips no more than ½ inch wide. Add to the salad and toss.

red cabbage, bean, and sausage salad with toasted fennel

1   **pound sweet Italian sausage**
1   **heaping tablespoon fennel seeds**
1   **small head red cabbage, about 1¼ pounds**
1   **15–ounce can cannellini beans**
6   **scallions**
1   **tablespoon Dijon mustard**
1   **tablespoon red wine vinegar**
¼   **cup extra–virgin olive oil**
     Salt and freshly ground black pepper

1   While the hot-water tap runs, put the sausages in a large, heavy skillet. Add 1 cup hot tap water, cover, and put over high heat. Cook for 5 to 6 minutes, depending on the thickness of the sausages. Uncover and cook for 5 to 6 minutes longer, until the water evaporates and the sausages are lightly browned and have no pink in the center. Turn the sausages once or twice to brown evenly.

2   Meanwhile, put the fennel seeds in a small heavy skillet over medium-low heat. Cook for 5 to 6 minutes, shaking the skillet occasionally, until the fennel becomes fragrant and lightly browned.

3   While the fennel seeds and sausage cook, halve the cabbage lengthwise and remove the core from each half. Shred the cabbage in a food processor with the shredding attachment. (Or shred using the large holes on a four-sided grater or a chef's knife.) You should have about 5 cups.

4   Put the cabbage in a large mixing bowl. Open the can of beans into a colander, rinse, and drain briefly. Trim the scallions and cut the white part and 2 inches of the green cross-wise into thin slices. Add the beans and scallions to the cabbage.

5   Mix the mustard, vinegar, oil, and salt and pepper to taste in a cup. Add the dressing and all but 1 teaspoon of the fennel seeds to the salad and toss well. Cut the cooked sausages crosswise into ⅜-inch-wide rounds, add to the salad, and toss well. Sprinkle with the remaining fennel seeds.

I usually think of red cabbage as the poor man's radicchio. It usually gets a supporting role in salads but here it has equal billing with beans and sausage. The toasted fennel brings all the elements together.

Serves 4

MAIL-ORDER SOURCES

COTÉ & COMPANY
800 North Easton Road
Doylestown, PA 18901
215-340-2683
Spanish piquillo, sweet red
peppers, Ortiz Spanish anchovies,
tuna packed in olive oil, olives,
olive oil, toasted sesame oil,
vinegar, cheeses, instant polenta,
pasta, instant couscous, basmati
rice, bulgur.

D'ARTAGNAN
280 Wilson Avenue
Newark, NJ 07105
800-327-8246; fax, 973-465-1870
Game birds, free-range poultry,
duck breasts, mergez and other
sausages.

DEAN & DELUCA
560 Broadway
New York, NY 10012
800-999-0306; fax, 212-334-6183
Olives, olive oil, toasted
sesame oil, vinegar, tuna packed
in olive oil, cheeses, instant
polenta, pasta, instant couscous,
basmati rice, bulgur, dried
black mission figs, spices.

KALUSTYAN'S
123 Lexington Avenue
New York, NY 10016
212-685-3451
Spices, fish sauce, toasted sesame
oil, basmati rice, instant polenta,
instant couscous, bulgur.

PENZEYS, LTD.
P.O. Box 933
Muskego, WI 53150
414-679-7207; fax, 414-679-7878
Herbs, spices, sesame seeds.

POLARICA
73 Hudson Street
New York, NY 10013
800-426-3487; fax, 718-706-1119
Game birds, free range chickens,
duck breasts, mergez sausage.

TODARO BROTHERS
555 Second Avenue
New York, NY 10016
212-532-0654
Spanish piquillo, sweet red
peppers, Ortiz Spanish anchovies,
tuna packed in olive oil, olives,
olive oil, vinegar, cheeses, dried
black mission figs, instant
polenta, pasta, basmati rice.

WILLIAMS-SONOMA
P.O. Box 7456
San Francisco, CA 94120-7456
800-541-2233; fax, 415-421-5153
Olive oil, walnut oil, hazelnut oil,
vinegar, sausages.

INDEX

TABLE OF EQUIVALENTS

The exact equivalents in the following tables have been rounded for convenience.

liquid and dry measures

U.S.	METRIC
¼ teaspoon	1.25 milliliters
½ teaspoon	2.5 milliliters
1 teaspoon	5 milliliters
1 tablespoon (3 teaspoons)	15 milliliters
1 fluid ounce (2 tablespoons)	30 milliliters
¼ cup	60 milliliters
⅓ cup	80 milliliters
1 cup	240 milliliters
1 pint (2 cups)	480 milliliters
1 quart (4 cups, 32 ounces)	960 milliliters
1 gallon (4 quarts)	3.84 liters
1 ounce (by weight)	28 grams
1 pound	454 grams
2.2 pounds	1 kilogram

length measures

U.S.	METRIC
⅛ inch	3 millimeters
¼ inch	6 millimeters
½ inch	12 millimeters
1 inch	2.5 centimeters

oven temperatures

FAHRENHEIT	CELSIUS	GAS
250	120	½
275	140	1
300	150	2
325	160	3
350	180	4
375	190	5
400	200	6
425	220	7
450	230	8
475	240	9
500	260	10